Uncertain Schema Matching

Uncertain Schema Matching

Avigdor Gal

ISBN: 978-3-031-00717-0   paperback
ISBN: 978-3-031-01845-9   ebook

DOI 10.1007/978-3-031-01845-9

A Publication in the Springer series
SYNTHESIS LECTURES ON DATA MANAGEMENT

Lecture #13
Series Editor: M. Tamer Özsu, *University of Waterloo*
Series ISSN
Synthesis Lectures on Data Management
Print 2153-5418   Electronic 2153-5426

Synthesis Lectures on Data Management

Editor
M. Tamer Özsu, *University of Waterloo*

Synthesis Lectures on Data Management is edited by Tamer Özsu of the University of Waterloo. The series will publish 50- to 125 page publications on topics pertaining to data management. The scope will largely follow the purview of premier information and computer science conferences, such as ACM SIGMOD, VLDB, ICDE, PODS, ICDT, and ACM KDD. Potential topics include, but not are limited to: query languages, database system architectures, transaction management, data warehousing, XML and databases, data stream systems, wide scale data distribution, multimedia data management, data mining, and related subjects.

Uncertain Schema Matching
Avigdor Gal
2011

Fundamentals of Object Databases: Object-Oriented and Object-Relational Design
Suzanne W. Dietrich and Susan D. Urban
2010

Advanced Metasearch Engine Technology
Weiyi Meng and Clement T. Yu
2010

Web Page Recommendation Models: Theory and Algorithms
Sule Gündüz-Ögüdücü
2010

Multidimensional Databases and Data Warehousing
Christian S. Jensen, Torben Bach Pedersen, and Christian Thomsen
2010

Database Replication
Bettina Kemme, Ricardo Jimenez Peris, and Marta Patino-Martinez
2010

Relational and XML Data Exchange
Marcelo Arenas, Pablo Barcelo, Leonid Libkin, and Filip Murlak
2010

User-Centered Data Management
Tiziana Catarci, Alan Dix, Stephen Kimani, and Giuseppe Santucci
2010

Data Stream Management
Lukasz Golab and M. Tamer Özsu
2010

Access Control in Data Management Systems
Elena Ferrari
2010

An Introduction to Duplicate Detection
Felix Naumann and Melanie Herschel
2010

Privacy-Preserving Data Publishing: An Overview
Raymond Chi-Wing Wong and Ada Wai-Chee Fu
2010

Keyword Search in Databases
Jeffrey Xu Yu, Lu Qin, and Lijun Chang
2009

Uncertain Schema Matching

Avigdor Gal
Technion – Israel Institute of Technology

SYNTHESIS LECTURES ON DATA MANAGEMENT #13

ABSTRACT

Schema matching is the task of providing correspondences between concepts describing the meaning of data in various heterogeneous, distributed data sources. Schema matching is one of the basic operations required by the process of data and schema integration, and thus has a great effect on its outcomes, whether these involve targeted content delivery, view integration, database integration, query rewriting over heterogeneous sources, duplicate data elimination, or automatic streamlining of workflow activities that involve heterogeneous data sources.

Although schema matching research has been ongoing for over 25 years, more recently a realization has emerged that schema matchers are inherently uncertain. Since 2003, work on the uncertainty in schema matching has picked up, along with research on uncertainty in other areas of data management.

This lecture presents various aspects of uncertainty in schema matching within a single unified framework. We introduce basic formulations of uncertainty and provide several alternative representations of schema matching uncertainty. Then, we cover two common methods that have been proposed to deal with uncertainty in schema matching, namely ensembles, and top-K matchings, and analyze them in this context. We conclude with a set of real-world applications.

KEYWORDS

schema matching, uncertainty, matcher ensembles, top-K schema matchings, data integration in peer-to-peer data management, Deep Web integration, data integration in disaster data management, Web service discovery and composition, and data integration for communities of knowledge

To my loving family:
Michal, Jonathan, and Natalie,
an island of certainty in an uncertain world.

Contents

Preface . . . . **xi**

1 Introduction **1**

   1.1 Schema Matching in the Data Integration Life Cycle 2

   1.2 Manuscript Outline 3

2 Models of Uncertainty **5**

   2.1 Probability Theory 5

   2.2 Fuzzy Set Theory 6

      2.2.1 Triangular Norms 6

      2.2.2 Fuzzy Aggregate Operators 7

   2.3 Discussion 8

3 Modeling Uncertain Schema Matching **9**

   3.1 Model 9

      3.1.1 Schema and attributes 10

      3.1.2 Attribute correspondences and the similarity matrix 11

      3.1.3 Schema matching 14

      3.1.4 (Yet Another) Schema Matcher Classification 15

   3.2 Model Usage 19

      3.2.1 Deep Web Information 19

      3.2.2 Semantic Matching 20

      3.2.3 Holistic Matching 20

      3.2.4 Non-$(1:1)$ cardinality constraints 21

   3.3 Reasoning with Uncertain Schema Matching 22

      3.3.1 Reasoning using Fuzzy Set Theory 22

      3.3.2 Reasoning using Probability Theory 26

   3.4 Assessing Matching Quality 27

      3.4.1 The monotonicity principle 29

4   Schema Matcher Ensembles **33**

4.1   The Art of Matcher Ensembling 33

4.2   2LNB: A Voting Mechanism for Ensembles 36

4.3   Constructing Ensembles 41

4.3.1   AdaBoost 42

4.3.2   SMB: Schema Matcher Boosting 43

4.3.3   Ensemble Construction with SMB: Empirical Analysis 46

5   Top-K Schema Matchings **49**

5.1   Top-K Schema Matchings: Definition 49

5.2   Algorithms for Identifying Top-K Matchings 51

5.2.1   Finding the Top-2 Matchings using A_{best} 51

5.2.2   Finding the Top-2 Matchings using Alternating Paths 52

5.2.3   Finding the Top-K Matchings 55

5.3   Extending top-K identification to Ensembles 60

5.3.1   The Matrix-Direct Algorithm 61

5.3.2   Matrix-Direct Algorithm with Bounding 63

5.4   Schema matching verification 65

5.5   Finding probabilistic attribute correspondences 69

6   Applications **71**

6.1   Peer-to-Peer Data Integration Systems 71

6.2   Disaster Data Management 72

6.3   Web Service Discovery and Composition 73

6.4   Communities of Knowledge 74

7   Conclusions and Future Work **75**

Author's Biography **85**

Preface

Schema matching is the task of providing correspondences between concepts describing the meaning of data in various heterogeneous, distributed data sources. Schema matching is one of the basic operations required by the process of data and schema integration, and thus has great effect on its outcomes. Schema matching research has been going on for more than 25 years now. The main objective of schema matchers is to provide correspondences that will be effective from the user's point of view, yet computationally efficient. Over the years, a realization has emerged that schema matchers are inherently uncertain. A matcher may consider several possible correspondences as possible, and when it needs to choose, it may choose wrong. A prime reason for the uncertainty of the matching process is the enormous ambiguity and heterogeneity of data description concepts: It is unrealistic to expect a single matcher to identify the correct mapping for any possible concept in a set. Since 2003, work on the uncertainty in schema matching has picked up (along with research on uncertainty in other areas of data management).

This manuscript presents various aspects of uncertainty in schema matching within a single unified framework. Chapter 2 introduces basic formulations of uncertainty, mainly from the AI literature. Here we discuss basic notions of probability theory and fuzzy set theory. For the former, we focus on possible worlds semantics, while for the latter, we introduce the notion of fuzzy relations.

Chapter 3 is devoted to several alternative representations of schema matching uncertainty. We present a typical model of the schema matching task and suggest probabilistic and fuzzy sets representations of the matching problem. We also discuss ways of assessing the quality of schema matchers, with a focus on a feature of schema matchers dubbed *monotonicity*. We show the relationship between monotonicity and a matcher's ability to correctly perform the matching task.

The next couple of chapters cover two common methods that have been proposed (either implicitly or explicitly) to deal with uncertainty in schema matching and analyze them in this context. Chapter 4 discusses matching by ensembles, considering a variety of matching alternatives as generated by multiple matchers. In particular, we shall focus on ensemble decision making using naïve Bayes and boosting mechanisms. Top-K schema matching will be discussed in Chapter 5. Here, instead of using multiple matchers, a single matcher (or ensemble) may be used to generate multiple alternative matchings. We shall discuss efficient methods for finding top-K matchings and for determining a consensus top-K in an ensemble, and we shall present a method for utilizing top-K matching to reduce the uncertainty in schema matching.

Chapter 6 provides a set of real-world applications where the modeling, reasoning, and algorithms to handle uncertain schema matchings can come into play. Finally, we conclude in Chapter 7 with an overview of challenges awaiting exploration by the research community.

This manuscript is based on much work performed by my devoted students, mainly Ateret Anaby-Tavor, Anan Marie, and Tomer Sagi. Much thanks is due to my colleagues Carmel Domshlak and Haggai Roitman. I would also like to thank Michael Katz and Nimrod Bussany for their assistance in reviewing early drafts and to Tamer Özsu who gave me the opportunity to lose so many hours of sleep in the manuscript creation process. It was definitely worth it. Finally, many thanks to my devoted technical editor, Meira Ben-Gad, for spending time (some of which, vacation time) in putting the final polish on this book.

Avigdor Gal

Faculty of Industrial Engineering & Management

Technion – Israel Institute of Technology

February 2011

CHAPTER 1

Introduction

> *Doubt is not a pleasant condition, but certainty is absurd.*
> – Voltaire

Schema matching is the task of providing correspondences between concepts describing the meaning of data in various heterogeneous, distributed data sources (*e.g.* attributes in database schemata, tags in XML DTDs, fields in HTML forms, input and output parameters in Web services, *etc.*). Schema matching is one of the basic operations required by the process of data and schema integration [Batini et al., 1986, Bernstein and Melnik, 2004, Lenzerini, 2002], and thus has great effect on its outcomes, whether these involve targeted content delivery, view integration, database integration, query rewriting over heterogeneous sources, duplicate data elimination, or automatic streamlining of workflow activities that involve heterogeneous data sources. As such, schema matching affects numerous modern applications from a wide variety of areas. It impacts business, where company data sources continuously realign due to changing markets; and it affects the way business and other information consumers seek information over the Web. It impacts the life sciences, where scientific workflows cross system boundaries more often than not. Finally, it impacts the way communities of knowledge are created and evolve.

Schema matching research has been going on for more than 25 years now, first as part of schema integration and then as a standalone research field (see surveys [Batini et al., 1986, Rahm and Bernstein, 2001, Sheth and Larson, 1990, Shvaiko and Euzenat, 2005] and online lists, *e.g.*, OntologyMatching[1] and Ziegler[2]). Over the years, a significant body of work has been devoted to the identification of *schema matchers*, heuristics for schema matching. The main objective of schema matchers is to provide correspondences that will be effective from the user's point of view, yet computationally efficient (or at least not disastrously expensive). Examples of algorithmic tools used for schema matching include COMA [Do and Rahm, 2002], Cupid [Madhavan et al., 2001], Onto-Builder [Gal et al., 2005b], Autoplex [Berlin and Motro, 2001], Similarity Flooding [Melnik et al., 2003], Clio [Miller et al., 2001], Glue [Doan et al., 2002], and others [Bergamaschi et al., 2001, Castano et al., 2001, Saleem et al., 2007]. These have come out of a variety of different research communities, including database management, information retrieval, the information sciences, data semantics and the semantic Web, and others. Research papers from different communities have

[1]http://www.ontologymatching.org/
[2]http://www.ifi.unizh.ch/~pziegler/IntegrationProjects.html

yielded overlapping, similar, and sometimes identical results. Meanwhile, benchmarks, such as the OAEI,[3] indicate that the performance of schema matchers still leaves something to be desired.

Over the years, a realization has emerged that schema matchers are inherently uncertain. A matcher may consider several possible correspondences as possible, and when it needs to choose, it may choose wrong [Gal, 2006]. For example, when two companies merge, the companies' employee databases need to be consolidated. The schemata may be different, and in such a case, there may be many different ways of mapping one schema to another. As another example, a Web search engine performing a product search over databases of multiple vendors needs to find correspondences between the product databases of different vendors. Multiple ways of representing the data might lead to multiple possible correspondences.

A prime reason for the uncertainty of the matching process is the enormous ambiguity and heterogeneity of data description concepts: It is unrealistic to expect a single matcher to identify the correct mapping for any possible concept in a set. Uncertainty in schema matching was recognized first in the form of anecdotal comments in research papers. Miller et al. [2000] justify uncertainty on the grounds that "the syntactic representation of schemas and data do not completely convey the semantics of different databases", *i.e.*, the description of a concept in a schema can be semantically misleading. In 2002, Madhavan et al. [2002] presented managing uncertainty in schema matching as the next issue on the research agenda in the realm of data integration. Since 2003, work on the uncertainty in schema matching has picked up (along with research on uncertainty in other areas of data management), with works such as those by Dong et al. [2007], Gal [2006], Gal et al. [2005a, 2009], Magnani et al. [2005] and Cheng et al. [2010].

1.1   SCHEMA MATCHING IN THE DATA INTEGRATION LIFE CYCLE

In 2004, Melnik and Bernstein offered a unique contribution to understanding the foundations of schema matching [Bernstein and Melnik, 2004, Melnik, 2004]. Their work proposes a conceptual framework of three layers, namely *applications*, *design patterns*, and *basic operators*. Of particular interest to this manuscript is the *match* operator, the operator that performs the schema matching. The matching operator precedes mapping operators, which provide an explicit representation of the functional relationships between attributes. Schema mapping typically incorporates the data transformation semantics required to migrate data from a source schema to a target schema, while the matching operator merely provides correspondences between attributes. Schema mapping has been researched heavily by Barbosa et al. [2005], Bohannon et al. [2005], Fagin [2006], and Fagin et al. [2007].

We focus on schema matching alone in this work. In some situations, matching and mapping can be performed jointly. However, this is not true in the general case. By concentrating on schema matching only, we aim to produce a clear and well-defined discussion that can serve as input to a

---

[3]http://www.om2006.ontologymatching.org/OAEI06/directory.htm

schema mapping process. It is worth noting that not all research works distinguish between matching and mapping. To maintain the coherence of the manuscript, in cases where our presentation is based on earlier works that refer to mapping, we adapt these to schema matching.

1.2   MANUSCRIPT OUTLINE

This manuscript presents various aspects of uncertainty in schema matching within a single unified framework. Chapter 2 introduces basic formulations of uncertainty, mainly from the AI literature. Here we discuss basic notions of probability theory and fuzzy set theory. For the former, we focus on possible worlds semantics, while for the latter, we introduce the notion of fuzzy relations.

Chapter 3 is devoted to several alternative representations of schema matching uncertainty. We present a typical model of the schema matching task and suggest probabilistic and fuzzy sets representations of the matching problem. We also discuss ways of assessing the quality of schema matchers, with a focus on a feature of schema matchers dubbed *monotonicity*. We show the relationship between monotonicity and a matcher's ability to correctly perform the matching task.

The next couple of chapters cover two common methods that have been proposed (either implicitly or explicitly) to deal with uncertainty in schema matching and analyze them in this context. Chapter 4 discusses matching by ensembles, considering a variety of matching alternatives as generated by multiple matchers. In particular we shall focus on ensemble decision making using naïve Bayes and boosting mechanisms. Top-K schema matching will be discussed in Chapter 5. Here, instead of using multiple matchers, a single matcher (or ensemble) may be used to generate multiple alternative matchings. We shall discuss efficient methods for finding top-K matchings and for determining a consensus top-K in an ensemble, and we shall present a method for utilizing top-K matching to reduce the uncertainty in schema matching.

Chapter 6 provides a set of real-world applications where the modeling, reasoning, and algorithms to handle uncertain schema matchings can come into play. Finally, we conclude in Chapter 7 with an overview of challenges awaiting exploration by the research community.

CHAPTER 2

Models of Uncertainty

> *Uncertainty is the refuge of hope.*
>   – Henri Frederic Amiel

The AI literature offers a rich body of work on modeling uncertainty, including, among others, studies on *lower and upper probabilities*, *Dempster-Shafer belief functions*, *possibility measures* (see [Halpern, 2003]), and *fuzzy sets* and *fuzzy logic* [Zadeh, 1965]. As an introduction to the modeling and handling of uncertainty in schema matching, we first present two common mechanisms for uncertainty management, namely probability theory and fuzzy set theory. According to Magnani and Montesi [2010], the former is representative of quantitative approaches in schema matching (*e.g.*, [Cheng et al., 2010, Dong et al., 2007, Gal et al., 2009]) and the latter of qualitative approaches (*e.g.*, [Gal et al., 2005a]). Other approaches for modeling uncertainty in schema matching include interval probabilities [Magnani et al., 2005], probabilistic datalog [Nottelmann and Straccia, 2005], possibilistic logic, and information loss estimation [Mena et al., 2000].

This chapter can be skipped if the reader is familiar with the basics of probability and fuzzy set theories. Also, it can be skipped at first reading, to be used as reference whenever the relevant theories are used in the text.

2.1 PROBABILITY THEORY

The most well-known and widely used framework for quantitative representation and reasoning about uncertainty is probability theory (see, *e.g.*, [Ross, 1997]). An intuitively appealing way to define a probability space involves possible world semantics [Green and Tannen, 2006]. Using such a definition, a probability space is a triple $pred = (W, F, \mu)$ such that:

- W is a set of possible worlds, with each possible world corresponding to a specific set of event occurrences that is considered possible. A typical assumption is that the real world is one of the possible worlds.

- $F \subseteq 2^{|W|}$ is a σ-algebra over W. σ-algebra, in general, and in particular F, is a nonempty collection of sets of possible worlds that is closed under complementation and countable unions. These properties of σ-algebra enable the definition of a probability space over F.

- $\mu : F \rightarrow [0, 1]$ is a probability measure over F.

We call the above representation of the probability space the *possible world representation*. In our context, each possible world is a set of attribute correspondences (see Section 3.1.2). One problem with possible worlds semantics is performance. Performing operations on possible worlds can lead to an exponential growth of alternatives. In this manuscript, we put an emphasis on efficient computation with possible worlds. In Chapter 5, we provide an efficient algorithm for generating the top-K most likely possible worlds (schema matchings). Chapter 4 analyzes the complexity of identifying a consensus possible world, given an ensemble of schema matchers.

2.2   FUZZY SET THEORY

The background on fuzzy set theory given here is based on the works of Gal et al. [2005a], Zadeh [1965], and Liu and Jacobsen [2004]. A *fuzzy set* M on a universe set U is a set that specifies, for each element $x \in U$, a degree of membership using a membership function

$$\mu_M : U \to [0, 1]$$

where $\mu_M(x) = \mu$ is the fuzzy membership degree of the element x in M. In what follows, we use μ^x to specify the element of interest whenever it cannot be clearly identified from the context. It is worth noting that, unlike in probability theory, the degree of membership of an element over all fuzzy sets M does not necessarily sum to 1.

We next present two families of operators, namely triangular norms (Section 2.2.1) and fuzzy aggregate operators (Section 2.2.2), that are commonly used in fuzzy sets theory, and compare their properties. Operators from both families are typically used in fuzzy-based applications to combine various fuzzy membership degrees. In Section 3.3.1, we demonstrate how fuzzy membership can be used to model the uncertainty of attribute correspondences using fuzzy relationships.

2.2.1   TRIANGULAR NORMS

The min operator is the most well-known representative of a large family of operators called *triangular norms* (t-norms, for short), routinely deployed as interpretations of fuzzy conjunctions (see, for example, the monographs of Klir and Yuan [1995] and Hajek [1998]). In the following, we define t-norms and discuss their relevant properties. We refer the interested reader to [Klement et al., 2000] for an exhaustive treatment of the subject.

A *triangular norm* $T : [0, 1] \times [0, 1] \to [0, 1]$ is a binary operator on the unit interval satisfying the following axioms for all $x, y, z \in [0, 1]$:

$$T(x, 1) = x \text{ (boundary condition)}$$
$$x \leq y \text{ implies } T(x, z) \leq T(y, z) \text{ (monotonicity)}$$
$$T(x, y) = T(y, x) \text{ (commutativity)}$$
$$T(x, T(y, z)) = T(T(x, y), z) \text{ (associativity)}$$

The following t-norm examples are typically used as interpretations of fuzzy conjunctions:

$$Tm(x, y) = \min(x, y) \text{ (minimum t-norm)}$$
$$Tp(x, y) = x \cdot y \text{ (product t-norm)}$$
$$Tl(x, y) = \max(x + y - 1, 0) \text{ (Lukasiewicz t-norm)}$$

It is worth noting that Tm is the only idempotent t-norm. That is, $Tm(x, x) = x$.[1] This becomes handy when comparing t-norms with fuzzy aggregate operators (Section 2.2.2). It can be easily proven (see [Hajek, 1998]) that

$$Tl(x, y) \leq Tp(x, y) \leq Tm(x, y)$$

for all $x, y \in [0, 1]$.

All t-norms over the unit interval can be represented as a combination of the triplet (Tm, Tp, Tl) (see [Hajek, 1998] for a formal presentation of this statement). For example, the Dubois-Prade family of t-norms T^{dp}, often used in fuzzy set theory and fuzzy logic, is defined using Tm, Tp and Tl as:

$$T^{dp}(x, y) = \begin{cases} \lambda \cdot Tp(\frac{x}{\lambda}, \frac{y}{\lambda}) & (x, y) \in [0, \lambda]^2 \\ Tm(x, y) & \text{otherwise} \end{cases}$$

2.2.2   FUZZY AGGREGATE OPERATORS

The *average* operator belongs to another large family of operators termed *fuzzy aggregate operators* [Klir and Yuan, 1995]. A fuzzy aggregate operator $H : [0, 1]^n \to [0, 1]$ satisfies the following axioms for every $x_1, \ldots, x_n \in [0, 1]$:

$$H(x_1, x_1, \ldots, x_1) = x_1 \text{ (idempotency)} \tag{2.1}$$
for every $y_1, y_2, \ldots, y_n \in [0, 1]$ such that $x_i \leq y_i$,
$$H(x_1, x_2, \ldots, x_n) \leq H(y_1, y_2, \ldots, y_n) \text{ (increasing monotonicity)} \tag{2.2}$$
$$H \text{ is a continuous function} \tag{2.3}$$

Let $\bar{x} = (x_1, \ldots, x_n)$ be a vector such that for all $1 \leq i \leq n$, $x_i \in [0, 1]$, and let $\bar{\varpi} = (\varpi_1, \ldots, \varpi_n)$ be a weight vector that sums to unity. Examples of fuzzy aggregate operators include the *average* operator $Ha(\bar{x}) = \frac{1}{n} \sum_1^n x_i$ and the *weighted average* operator $Hwa(\bar{x}, \bar{\varpi}) = \bar{x} \cdot \bar{\varpi}$. Clearly, *average* is a special case of the *weighted average* operator, where $\varpi_1 = \cdots = \varpi_n = \frac{1}{n}$. It is worth noting that Tm (the min t-norm) is also a fuzzy aggregate operator, due to its idempotency (its associative property provides a way of defining it over any number of arguments). However, Tp and Tl are not fuzzy aggregate operators.

T-norms and fuzzy aggregate operators are comparable, using the following inequality:

$$\min(x_1, \ldots, x_n) \leq H(x_1, \ldots, x_n)$$

for all $x_1, \ldots, x_n \in [0, 1]$ and function H satisfying axioms 2.1-2.3.

---

[1] For a binary operator f, idempotency is defined to be $f(x, x) = x$ (similar to Klir and Yuan [1995], p. 36).

2.3   DISCUSSION

Probabilistic and fuzzy set theories are competing methods for modeling uncertainty. A probabilistic-based approach assumes that one has incomplete knowledge about the portion of the real world being modeled. However, this knowledge can be encoded as probabilities about events. The fuzzy approach, on the other hand, aims at modeling the intrinsic imprecision of features of the modeled reality. Therefore, the amount of knowledge at the user's disposal is of little concern. Also, probabilistic reasoning typically relies on event independence assumptions, making correlated events harder (and sometimes impossible) to assess. Drakopoulos [1995] presents a comparative study of the capabilities of probability and fuzzy methods. This study shows that probabilistic analysis is intrinsically more expressive than fuzzy sets. However, fuzzy methods demonstrate higher computational efficiency.

   In this book, we do not aim at determining whether one representation is better than the other. Rather, we show how to use both approaches for modeling the uncertainty of attribute correspondences and schema matchings. We also show how reasoning can be done with each of these approaches.

CHAPTER 3

Modeling Uncertain Schema Matching

Concepts cannot be identical with mental objects of any kind.
– Hilary Putnam

Theoretical models for attribute correspondences have been investigated by Alagic and Bernstein [2001], Madhavan et al. [2002], and Benerecetti et al. [2005]. Alagic and Bernstein [2001] represent correspondences using morphisms (structure-preserving mappings) in categories (which can be viewed as typed objects) [Lane, 1998]. The work of Madhavan et al. [2002] provides explicit semantics for matchings using logical models and model satisfaction. Benerecetti et al. [2005] provide a formal model of schema matching for topic hierarchies, modeled as rooted directed trees, where a node has a "meaning" generated using an ontology. A matching connects topic hierarchies by some relation (*e.g.*, subsumption).

In this chapter, we seek a generic data model for representing the uncertainty of the matching process. Our proposed model allows the modeling of uncertainty while seeking better algorithms to reduce it (and thus increase user effectiveness), and supporting features such as matcher ensembling. We start by presenting a schema matching model in Section 3.1. In Section 3.2, we demonstrate, using several examples, that the similarity matrix is sufficient for modeling basic uncertainty of correspondences. Then, we discuss two alternatives to reasoning with uncertainty in schema matching: fuzzy-set theory in Section 3.3.1 and probability theory in Section 3.3.2. We conclude with a description of how schema matchers are assessed for quality (Section 3.4).

3.1 MODEL

We now provide a model for schema matching, drawing on various ideas from the literature, and show its wide applicability and usability. We accompany the description with an example, based on [Gal, 2010].

Example 3.1   This case study involves the design of a hotel reservation portal. The portal merges various information databases for the hotel chain RoomsRUs, adding a mashup application that helps position the hotels on a geographical map. We consider three relational databases. Database R contains three relations: credit card information in the CardInfo relation; hotel information in

Table 3.1: Sample Database Schema Description					
Database R					
CardInfo	type	cardNum	lastName	firstName	securityCode
	expiryMonth	expiryYear			
HotelInfo	hotelName	neighborhood	city		
Reservations	cardNum	lastName	firstName	arrivalDate	departureDate
Database S					
CardInformation	type	cardNum	securityCode	expiryMonth	expiryYear
HotelCardInformation	clientNum	expiryMonth	expiryYear		
ReserveDetails	clientNum	name	checkInDay	checkOutDay	
Database T					
CityInfo	city	neighborhood	GPSPosition		
Subway	city	station	GPSPosition		

the **HotelInfo** relation; and reservation information in the relation **Reservations**. Database S also stores credit card information, distinguishing between hotel credit cards and major credit cards. Therefore, S contains the following three relations, **CardInformation** and **HotelCardInformation**. It also contains reservation information in the relation **ReserveDetails**. Finally, database T has two relations, **CityInfo** and **Subway**. **CityInfo** provides information about neighborhoods where the hotels are located and their approximate GPS positioning. **Subway** provides similar information for subway stations. A partial description of the databases appears in Table 3.1.   □

3.1.1   SCHEMA AND ATTRIBUTES

Let *schema* $S = \{A_1, A_2, ..., A_n\}$ be a finite set of *attributes*. Attributes can be both simple and compound, and compound attributes should not necessarily be disjoint. An attribute in a schema of a hotel reservation Web site might be lastName, firstName, *etc.* A compound attribute might be creditCardInfo, combining three other attributes—type, cardNum, and expiry (which could itself be a compound attribute, representing month and year of expiration). A question that immediately presents itself is whether such a simple representation of a schema is sufficient for our purposes. Clearly, metadata models use more complex representations; relational databases use tables and foreign keys, XML structures have hierarchies, OWL ontologies contain general axioms, *etc.* However, keeping in mind that we aim at modeling the uncertainty in matching attributes, no richer representation of data models is needed. For instance, if we aim at matching simple attributes such as lastName and firstName, we need not represent their composition in a compound attribute called name. If the goal of our schema matching process is to match compound structures such as XML paths (see, *e.g.*, [Vinson et al., 2007]), then XML paths are the elements we define as attributes in our schemata. Clearly, we need to justify our decision, and show that we do not lose precious semantic information in the translation process. We defer this discussion to Section 3.2.

3.1.2   ATTRIBUTE CORRESPONDENCES AND THE SIMILARITY MATRIX

Let S and S' be schemata with n and n' attributes, respectively.[1] Let $\mathcal{S} = S \times S'$ be the set of all possible *attribute correspondences* between S and S'. $\mathcal{S}$ is a set of attribute pairs (*e.g.*, (arrivalDate, checkInDay)). Let $M\left(S, S'\right)$ be an $n \times n'$ *similarity matrix* over $\mathcal{S}$, where $M_{i,j}$ represents a degree of similarity between the i-th attribute of S and the j-th attribute of S'. The majority of works in the schema matching literature define $M_{i,j}$ to be a real number in $(0, 1)$. $M\left(S, S'\right)$ is a *binary similarity matrix* if for all $1 \leq i \leq n$ and $1 \leq j \leq n'$, $M_{i,j} \in \{0, 1\}$. That is, a binary similarity matrix accepts only 0 and 1 as possible values.

Table 3.2: A Similarity Matrix Example

$S_1 \longrightarrow$ $\downarrow S_2$	1 cardNum	2 city	3 arrivalDate	4 departureDate
1 clientNum	0.843	0.323	0.317	0.302
2 city	0.290	1.000	0.326	0.303
3 checkInDay	0.344	0.328	0.351	0.352
4 checkOutDay	0.312	0.310	0.359	0.356

Table 3.3: A Binary Similarity Matrix Example

$S_1 \longrightarrow$ $\downarrow S_2$	1 cardNum	2 city	3 arrivalDate	4 departureDate
1 clientNum	1	0	0	0
2 city	0	1	0	0
3 checkInDay	0	0	0	1
4 checkOutDay	0	0	1	0

Example 3.2   Consider tables 3.2 and 3.3, representing simplified similarity matrices of the running case study. The similarity matrix in Table 3.2 is a simplified version of the matching between two schemata of Example 3.1. The similarity matrix in Table 3.3 is a binary similarity matrix. Matrix elements are given using both attribute names and numbers.   □

Similarity matrices are generated by schema matchers. *Schema matchers* are instantiations of the schema matching process. They differ mainly in the measures of similarity they employ, which yield different similarity matrices. These measures can be arbitrarily complex, and may use various techniques. Some matchers assume similar attributes are more likely to have similar names [He and Chang, 2003, Su et al., 2006]. Other matchers assume similar attributes share similar domains [Gal et al., 2005b, Madhavan et al., 2001]. Others yet take instance similarity as an indication

---

[1]For ease of exposition, we constrain our presentation to a matching process involving two schemata. Extensions to holistic schema matching are discussed in Section 3.2.

of attribute similarity [Berlin and Motro, 2001, Doan et al., 2001]. Finally, some researchers use the experience of previous matchings as indicators of attribute similarity [He and Chang, 2005, Madhavan et al., 2005, Su et al., 2006].

Example 3.3   To illustrate our model, and for the sake of completeness, we now present a few examples of schema matchers, representative of many other, similar matchers. Detailed descriptions of these matchers can be found in [Gal et al., 2005b] and [Marie and Gal, 2007a]:

Term: Term matching compares attribute names to identify syntactically similar attributes. To achieve better performance, names are preprocessed using several techniques originating in IR research. Term matching is based on either complete words or string comparison. As an example, consider the relations CardInfo and HotelCardInformation, which we refer to as compound attributes herein. The maximum common substring is CardInfo, and the similarity of the two terms is $\frac{length(\text{CardInfo})}{length(\text{HotelCardInformation})} = \frac{8}{20} = 40\%$.

Value: Value matching utilizes domain constraints (*e.g.*, drop lists, check boxes, and radio buttons). It becomes valuable when comparing two attributes whose names do not match exactly. For example, consider attributes arrivalDate and checkInDay. These two attributes have associated value sets {(*Select*),*1,2,...,31*} and {(*Day*),*1,2,...,31*}, respectively, and thus their content-based similarity is $\frac{31}{33} = 94\%$, which is significantly higher than their term similarity ($\frac{2(\text{Da})}{11(\text{arrivalDate})} = 18\%$).

Composition: A composite attribute is composed of other attributes (either atomic or composite). Composition can be translated into a hierarchy. This schema matcher assigns similarity to attributes based on the similarity of their neighbors. The Cupid matcher [Madhavan et al., 2001], for example, is based on attribute composition.

Precedence: The order in which data are provided in an interactive process is important. In particular, data given at an earlier stage may restrict the options for a later entry. For example, when filling in a form on a hotel reservation site, available room types can be determined using the information given regarding location and check-in time. Once those entries are filled in, the information is sent back to the server and the next form is brought up. Such precedence relationships can usually be identified by the activation of a script, such as the one associated with a SUBMIT button. Precedence relationships can be translated into a precedence graph. The matching algorithm is based on a technique dubbed *graph pivoting*, as follows. When matching two attributes, each is considered to be a pivot within its own schema, thus partitioning the graph into a subgraph of all preceding and all succeeding attributes. By comparing preceding subgraphs and succeeding subgraphs, the confidence strength of the pivot attributes is determined. Precedence was used by Su [2007] to determine attribute correspondences with a holistic matcher.   □

It was hypothesized and empirically validated by Marie and Gal [2007b] that when encoding attribute pair similarities in a similarity matrix, a matcher would be inclined to assign a value of 0 to each pair it conceives not to match, and a similarity measure higher than 0 (and probably closer to 1) to those attribute pairs that are conceived to be correct. This tendency, however, is masked by "noise," whose sources are rooted in missing and uncertain information. Therefore, instead of expecting a binary similarity matrix, with a 0 score for all incorrect attribute mappings and a unit score for all attribute correspondences, the values in a similarity matrix form two probability distributions over [0, 1], one for incorrect attribute mappings (with higher density around 0), and another for correct attribute correspondences.

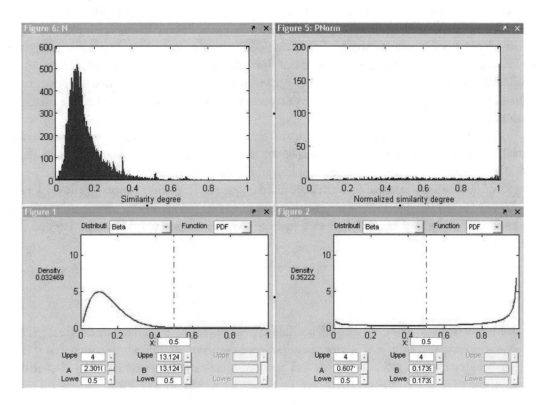

Figure 3.1: Illustration of a matcher's behavior

Figure 3.1 (presented first by Marie and Gal [2007b]) illustrates schema matcher behavior, based on an evaluation of more than 26,239 attribute pairs coming from 50 schema pairs. The top left box in Figure 3.1 shows a distribution with a higher density around 0, representing the similarity values that were assigned to incorrect attribute correspondences by the precedence matcher. The top right box of Figure 3.1 reflects a set of normalized similarity values of correct attribute correspondences. Normalization was achieved by dividing all similarity values in a matrix by the highest value in that matrix. The two boxes at the bottom of Figure 3.1 were generated using a beta distribution. According to Ross [1997]: "The beta distribution can be used to model a random phenomenon whose set of possible values is in some finite interval $[c, d]$—which, by letting c denote the origin and taking $d - c$ as a unit measurement, can be transformed into the interval $[0, 1]$." A beta distribution has two tuning parameters, a and b. To receive a density function that is skewed to the left (as in the case of incorrect attribute correspondences, bottom left in Figure 3.1), we require that $b > a$. For right-skewed density functions (as in the case of correct attribute correspondences, bottom right), one needs to set $a > b$.

Going back to the semantics of data models, we note that schema matchers often use data model semantics when determining the similarity between attributes. For example, XML structure has been used in Cupid [Madhavan et al., 2001] to support or dispute linguistic similarities. Also, the similarity flooding algorithm [Melnik et al., 2002] uses structural links between attributes to update linguistic similarities. However, once this similarity has been determined and recorded in the similarity matrix, the original semantics that derived it is no longer needed. Therefore, the matrix representation, as given above, is sufficient to represent the uncertainty involved in the matching process.

Similarity matrices have been used in the literature mainly as a convenient representation model, rather than a formal model that is used for reasoning, with two exceptions. Do and Rahm [2002] propose a cube to represent an ensemble of similarity values, transformed into a matrix by aggregating the similarity values of each attribute matching across ensemble members. Domshlak et al. [2007] have taken this process one step further and proposed the use of the matrix abstraction to perform local and global aggregations as a matrix-to-constant and cube-to-matrix function (see Chapter 4).

3.1.3   SCHEMA MATCHING

Let the power-set $\Sigma = 2^S$ be the set of all possible *schema matchings* between the schema pair (S, S'), where a schema matching $\sigma \in \Sigma$ is a set of attribute correspondences. It is worth noting that σ does not necessarily contain all attributes in S or S'. Therefore, there may exist an attribute $A \in S$, such that for all $A' \in S', (A, A') \notin \sigma$. For convenience, we denote by $\bar{\sigma} = \{A \in S \,|\, \forall A' \in S', (A, A') \notin \sigma\} \cup \{A' \in S' \,|\, \forall A \in S, (A, A') \notin \sigma\}$ the set of all attributes that do not participate in a schema matching.

Let $\Gamma : \Sigma \to \{0, 1\}$ be a boolean function that captures the application-specific constraints on schema matchings, *e.g.*, cardinality constraints and inter-attribute correspondence constraints. Γ partitions Σ into two sets, where the set of all *valid* schema matchings in Σ is given by $\Sigma_\Gamma = \{\sigma \in \Sigma \,|\, \Gamma(\sigma) = 1\}$. Γ is a general constraint model, where $\Gamma(\sigma) = 1$ means that the matching σ can be accepted by a designer. Γ has been modeled in the literature using special types of matchers called *constraint enforcers* [Lee et al., 2007], whose output is recorded in a binary similarity matrix. We say Γ is a *null constraint function* (basically accepting all possible matchings as valid with no use of a constraint enforcer) if for all $\sigma \in \Sigma, \Gamma(\sigma) = 1$.

The input to the process of schema matching is given by two schemata S and S' and a constraint boolean function Γ. The output of the schema matching process is a *schema matching* $\sigma \in \Sigma_\Gamma$. To illustrate, consider the examples in tables 3.2 and 3.3. The similarity matrix in Table 3.2 represents a step in the schema matching process, in which the similarity of attribute correspondences is recorded in a similarity matrix. Table 3.3 presents a possible outcome of the matching process, where all attribute correspondences, for which a value of 1 is assigned, are part of the resulting schema matching. The constraint function that is applied in this example enforces a $1:1$ matching.

By now, it has become apparent that we conceive the matrix abstraction to be a suitable model of uncertain schema matching. Therefore, we take our approach one step further and provide a formalization of the matching process output using similarity matrices.

Definition 3.4 Matrix Satisfaction Let $M\left(S, S'\right)$ be an $n \times n'$ similarity matrix over $\mathcal{S}$. A schema matching $\sigma \in \Sigma$ is said to *satisfy* $M\left(S, S'\right)$ (denoted $\sigma \models M\left(S, S'\right)$) if $\left(A_i, A'_j\right) \in \sigma \to M_{i,j} > 0$. $\sigma \in \Sigma_\Gamma$ is said to *maximally satisfy* $M\left(S, S'\right)$ if $\sigma \models M\left(S, S'\right)$ and for each $\sigma' \in \Sigma_\Gamma$ such that $\sigma' \models M\left(S, S'\right), \sigma' \subset \sigma$.

The output of a schema matching is therefore a similarity matrix $M\left(S, S'\right)$. An attribute pair $\left(A_i, A_j\right)$ can be considered an attribute correspondence in the output schema matching only $M\left(i', j\right) > 0$. A schema matching σ satisfies M if the above is true for any attribute pair in σ. Finally, we define the output of the schema matching process to be a valid schema matching that **maximally** satisfies $M\left(S, S'\right)$.

Schema matching satisfaction, just like Γ, partitions Σ into two sets. In the case of the former, the partitioning is based on the matching requirements, while in the latter, it is based on the application and the matcher's ability to determine attribute requirements. Therefore, the partitioning induced by Γ does not necessarily overlap with that induced by the satisfaction criterion and may, at times, be at odds with it. It is easy to see that in the absence of a constraint function Γ, *i.e.*, whenever $\Sigma_\Gamma = \Sigma$ or whenever Γ is ignored by the matcher, there is exactly one schema matching that maximally satisfies M. This schema matching is that which contains all attribute correspondences $\left(A_i, A'_j\right)$ for which $M_{i,j} > 0$. However, when Γ is both meaningful and used by the matcher, there may be more than a single valid schema matching that maximally satisfies M. For example, if a $1:1$ constraint is enforced, there may be several schema matchings that neither contain nor are contained by others that satisfy the condition of maximal satisfaction. Similarly, if none of the valid schema matchings satisfy M then, clearly, the matcher yields no schema matching as an outcome of the matching process.

3.1.4 (YET ANOTHER) SCHEMA MATCHER CLASSIFICATION

At first glance, the idea of defining matrix satisfaction seems odd. We have shown in Section 3.1.2 that in most cases schema matchers will not decisively assign a value of 0 to any attribute pair matching. Taking Definition 3.4 at its face value is likely to result in any attribute pair being declared an attribute correspondence. Moreover, when using the definition of maximum satisfaction, constraints may be violated. For example, many matrices will violate a 1 : 1 schema matching constraint, as they have so many non-zero entries.

To enhance our understanding of uncertainty in schema matching, and the validity of Definition 3.4, we now define *second-line matchers* (2LM) [Gal and Sagi, 2010]. A 2LM is a schema matcher whose inputs are no longer the schemata S and S', but rather a similarity matrix $M(S, S')$ (together with Γ).

Definition 3.5   Given schemata S and S', we denote by $\mathcal{M}(S, S')$ the (possibly infinite) set of similarity matrices $M(S, S')$. A second-line schema matcher

$$SM : \mathcal{M}(S, S')^+ \times \Gamma \to \mathcal{M}(S, S')$$

is a mapping, transforming one (or more) similarity matrices into another similarity matrix.

Second-line schema matchers operate solely on similarity matrices. In contrast, we term non-2LM as *first-line schema matchers* (1LM), matchers that operate on the schemata themselves, using semantics of the application. For example, a linguistic matcher is a 1LM, using attribute names or descriptions in matching attributes. One can envision a 2LM that receives as an input the similarity matrix that was generated by the linguistic matcher and improves it, *e.g.*, by thresholding or by combining it with a matrix of another matcher.

Example 3.6   In Example 3.3, we introduced several matchers, all of which fall into the category of first-line matchers. Two simple examples of second-line matchers are the following:

Term **and** Value: A weighted combination of the Term and Value matchers. Here, the input to the matcher involves similarity matrices.

Combined: A weighted combination of the Term, Value, Composition, and Precedence matchers.

The following are additional second-line matchers that are based on constraint satisfaction:

- The Maximum Weighted Bipartite Graph (MWBG) algorithm and the Stable Marriage (SM) algorithm both enforce a cardinality constraint of 1 : 1. The former uses a bipartite graph, where nodes in each side of the graph represent attributes of one of the schemata, and the weighted edges represent the similarity measures between attributes. Algorithms such as those presented in Galil [1986] provide the output of the MWBG heuristic. The latter takes a similarity matrix and applies a stable marriage algorithm [Gusfield and Irving, 1989] to identify a schema matching. Marie and Gal [2007a] have introduced a heuristic dubbed Intersection that simply computes and outputs the intersection set of both algorithm outputs. For the sake of completeness, we should also mention the Union matcher, which includes in the output matching any attribute correspondence that is in the output of either MWBG or SM. All four matchers (MWBG, SM, Intersection, and Union) are second-line matchers. It is worth noting that neither Intersection nor Union enforces 1 : 1 matching.

- A variation of the SM matcher is the Dominants matcher. This matcher chooses *dominant pairs*, those pairs in the similarity matrix with maximum value in both their row and their column. The main assumption guiding this heuristic is that the dominant pairs are the most likely to be attribute correspondences since the two attributes involved in a dominant pair prefer each other most. It is worth noting that with this heuristic not all the target attributes are mapped and that an attribute in one schema may be mapped to more than one attribute in another schema, whenever attribute pairs share the same similarity level.

- Finally, Marie and Gal [2007b] have introduced 2LNB, a 2LM that uses a naïve Bayes classifier over matrices to determine attribute correspondences. Autoplex [Berlin and Motro, 2001], LSD [Doan et al., 2001], iMAP [Dhamankar et al., 2004], and sPLMap [Nottelmann and Straccia, 2007] also use a naïve Bayes classifier to learn attribute correspondence probabilities using an instance training set. 2LNB is the only 2LM in this group.□

We now provide two more examples of second-line matchers, highlighting the differences in their modus operandi from first-line matchers.

Example 3.7 eTuner A model of a 1 : 1 matching system was defined by Lee et al. [2007] to be a triple, one element being a library of matching components. This library has four types of components, namely Matcher, Combiner, Constraint Enforcer, and Match Selector. The first type is a 1LM, in its classical definition. The remaining three types are second-line schema matchers according to our definition.

A *combiner* [Do and Rahm, 2002] follows the definition of a schema matcher with a null constraint function, *i.e.*, there are no constraints on the set of attribute correspondences in the output. A combination can be made by aggregating elements of the input matrices or by using machine learning techniques such as stacking and decision trees.

A *constraint enforcer* is simply a 2LM (note that our definition in Section 3.1.3 allows adding constraints at first-line matchers as well).

A *match selector* returns a matrix in which all elements that are not selected are reduced to 0. Two examples are given by Lee et al. [2007]: thresholding and the use of the MWBG algorithm for selecting a maximum weighted bipartite graph.   □

Example 3.8 Top-*K* A heuristic that utilizes the top-*K* best schema matchings to produce an improved schema matching was proposed by Gal [2006] and will be described in depth in Section 5.4. It is a special type of a combiner and a match selector, in which the input does not come from different matchers (as is generally done with ensembles [Bernstein et al., 2004, Embley et al., 2002, Gal et al., 2005b, Mork et al., 2006]). Rather, the same schema matcher generates multiple matrices that are then evaluated to generate a single similarity matrix by a special form of thresholding.   □

Comparing examples 3.7 and 3.8 raises interesting observations. First, the modeling of second-line matchers can serve as a reference framework for comparing various research efforts in schema matching. For example, while combiners and match selectors are defined to be separate types by Lee et al. [2007], they were combined and redefined by Gal [2006]. A second observation involves the goal of second-line matchers. Second-line matchers aim at improving the outcomes of first-line schema matchers, increasing their robustness. This idea is appealing since complementary matchers can potentially compensate for each other's weaknesses [Bernstein et al., 2004]. Gal [2006] has shown that the use of a heuristic, based on top-K best schema matchings, has increased the precision of mappings by 25% on average, at the cost of a minor 8% reduction in recall.

Table 3.4: Two dimension matcher classification		
Matcher	**First-Line Matcher**	**Second-Line Matcher**
Non-decisive	Term	Combined
Decision maker		MWBG

We now propose yet another classification of matchers on two orthogonal dimensions (see Table 3.4 for classification and example matchers). The first dimension separates first- from second-line schema matchers. The second dimension separates those matchers that aim at specifying schema matchings, dubbed *decision makers*, from those that compute similarity values yet do not make decisions at the schema level. Using Definition 3.5, we can say that a matcher is decisive if it satisfies Γ. The most common type is a non-decisive first-line matcher. The OntoBuilder's Term matcher belongs to this class, as does a WordNet-based decision tree technique proposed by Embley et al. [2002]. Combiners, in COMA's terminology, are non-decisive second-line schema matchers. They combine similarity matrices of other matchers, and hence they are second-line matchers by definition. However, their similarity matrix is not meant to be used to decide on a single schema matching.

Well-known decisive second-line matchers are algorithms like MWBG and SM. Both algorithms fall into the category of constraint enforcers as described by Lee et al. [2007], and both enforce a cardinality constraint of 1 : 1. Finally, the class of first-line decision makers contains few if any matchers. The main reason for this is that most systems abide by the long conceptual modeling tradition of database schema integration, as summarized by Batini et al. [1986]: "The comparison activity focuses on primitive objects first…; then it deals with those modeling constructs that represent associations among primitive objects." This dichotomy has in the main been preserved in schema matching as well.

As a concluding remark, we compare the proposed classification with the classifications of Rahm and Bernstein [2001] and Euzenat and Shvaiko [2007]. Rahm and Bernstein [2001] partition matchers into *individual matchers* and *combining matchers*. The latter class contains only second-line schema matchers. Individual matchers can also serve as second-line matchers. For example, a matcher that takes the outcome of another matcher and applies a threshold condition on it is an *individual, second-line* matcher. Combining matchers are further partitioned into composite and hybrid matchers, a classification that is less relevant in our classification system, where the secondary partitioning is based on the decisiveness of a matcher. The *alignments as solutions* class of Euzenat and Shvaiko [2007] is the same as *second-line decisive* matchers, and the class of *alignments as likeness clues* contains the class of *non-decisive matchers* (whether they be first- or second-line). No special treatment is given to the separation of matchers that make use of application semantics from those that rely solely on the outcomes of previous matchers.

3.2   MODEL USAGE

We propose to use the matrix abstraction to model uncertainty in the schema matching process. The matrix is a natural representation for the outcome of schema matchers, and it has been used in many previous works. However, beyond its appealing representation, the theoretical model underlying matrix operations make it a good candidate for manipulating the similarity measures. Therefore, basic matching operations will be captured as matrix operations, regardless of whether the matcher itself is using a linguistic heuristic, a machine learning heuristic, etc. Furthermore, existing matrix properties will be used to analyze matcher performance, as reflected in their matrix representation.

To demonstrate the usability of this model, we present four examples to show the wide applicability of the similarity matrix as a model for uncertainty in schema matching. It is worth noting that the use of matrices as the basic model for uncertainty in schema matching opens a vast and well-established area—one that has been studied for many generations—for research in the design of schema matching algorithms. Clearly, the few works that have used similarity matrices beyond a convenient representation model have not even scratched the surface in using matrix theory to seek better schema matchers.

3.2.1   DEEP WEB INFORMATION

We start with a very simple example, involving the matching of deep Web information. The deep Web hides information behind Web forms. Typically, this information is stored in databases on the server side. While the database schemata are not known, the information they contain, which is exposed to users via Web forms, can be extracted and matched. Several works focus on deep Web information matching, including He and Chang [2003] and Gal et al. [2005b]. As the main task of the matching process is to match form fields, matrix rows represent the fields of one form and matrix columns those of the other. Each entry in the matrix represents the similarity of two fields. In OntoBuilder, such a similarity can be attributed to linguistic similarity of labels (the text that surrounds the field), linguistic similarity of field names (identifiers that are sent to the server when a form is filled in), domain similarity (similarities in the set of acceptable values), and structural similarities.

Two examples of structural similarities are supported by OntoBuilder [Gal et al., 2005b]. First, fields may be composed under a single label—*e.g.*, the field associated with the attribute arrivalDate is labeled "Please specify your arrival date" in a Web form. This may represent a composite attribute with three fields corresponding to check-in day, month, and year. The second structural similarity is based on a precedence relationship, as detailed in Example 3.3.

Although the analysis of schemata may be rich, as illustrated above, its translation to a similarity matrix is lossless. Each type of similarity is captured in a separate similarity matrix—*e.g.*, one similarity matrix will encode the linguistic similarities and another will capture the precedence similarity. These matrices represent first-line matchers and can later be combined using a second-line matcher.

Another observation from this case study is that a row or column in a similarity matrix can represent a composite attribute (*e.g.*, **Please specify your arrival date**) or each of its components. In the latter case, we will have three rows/columns corresponding to check-in day, month, and year.

3.2.2   SEMANTIC MATCHING

As another example, consider the model of semantic matching, in the realm of the semantic Web [Euzenat and Shvaiko, 2007], where pairwise matching results in an ontological relationship (*e.g.*, equivalence and subsumption) between attributes rather than quantification of similarity measures. In this case, for each pair of elements only one relationship holds. The S-Match system [Giunchiglia et al., 2005] takes two graph-like structures (*e.g.*, XML schemata) as input and generates a confidence measure to attribute pairs (using concept comparison) from which one ontological relationship is chosen. Therefore, taking a pair of attributes, each from a different schema, S-Match generates a confidence measure for their semantic relationship being equivalence, subsumption, *etc.* Then, a single relationship is chosen for each attribute pair.

Such a model is easily captured by the matrix model given here. Each ontological relationship is modeled as a separate matrix (one matrix for equivalence, one for subsumption, *etc.*). These matrices represent the confidence level in an ontological relationship. A second-line matcher (specific to S-Match) then generates a set of binary matrices, where 1 represents the existence of a relationship and 0 represents no relationship, using some thresholds. During this process, and as part of a constraint enforcer, if the same entry in two matrices is computed to be 1, a lattice structure (where, for example, equivalence is higher than subsumption) determines which values are to remain 1 and which will be lowered to 0. As a final step, any entry for which a 0 value is recorded in all matrices is assigned 1 for the *idk* (stands for "I don't know") matrix. Such modeling may be of much practical value, especially if semantic matching is combined with quantity-based methods (*e.g.*, based on string matching) to create matcher ensembles.

3.2.3   HOLISTIC MATCHING

A third example involves holistic matching, which has been discussed mainly by He and Chang [2005] and Su et al. [2006]. Rather than matching two schemata at a time, holistic matching matches multiple schemata in an attempt to reach a consensus terminology for a domain. Madhavan et al. [2005] use a corpus that may be considered an outcome of a holistic matching to improve the matching to a new schema.

A natural representation of holistic matching would employ multi-dimensional matrices. As an example, consider the holistic matching of three schemata. Instead of a 2-dimensional matrix, we use a 3-dimensional matrix where each entry represents the certainty of three attributes, one from each schema, being matched.

3.2.4   NON-$(1 : 1)$ CARDINALITY CONSTRAINTS

Finally, we discuss the role of similarity matrices in enforcing non-$1 : 1$ cardinality constraints. This discussion is mainly based on Gal [2005]. Consider, for example, a scenario presented by Miller et al. [2001], in which attribute sal from relation Professor is combined with attributes hrrate and workson from relation payrate, to compute the attribute sal in the Personnel relation. Can a similarity matrix support such a matching? The answer to this question is yes, and there are two ways to do so, based on the abilities of the schema matcher.

The assignment of similarity measures to non-$1 : 1$ attribute correspondences can be defined in a variety of ways. First, let's assume that the matching algorithm can provide a similarity score for the matching of groups of attributes. Therefore, when matching name with firstName and lastName, we can have four different similarity measures, one for matching name with lastName, another for matching name with firstName, and two more for matching name with ⟨firstName, lastName⟩ and ⟨lastName, firstName⟩. The similarity matrix will then have additional rows or columns to represent the extra complexity of the matching task. The increase in the matrix size depends on the Γ constraint function. For example, if the matching constraint allows a single attribute in one schema to be matched with up to **two** attributes in another schema, one needs to consider all possible pairs in a schema. Therefore, n_1 elements of one schema are matched with $\begin{pmatrix} n_2 \\ 2 \end{pmatrix} = \frac{1}{2} n_2 (n_2 - 1)$ elements of the other schema. This computation can be generalized to any (sufficiently small) constant c, constraining the number of attributes in an element. The complexity in this case is of $\mathcal{O}(n^c)$. It is worth noting that with such a solution, an algorithm for enforcing a $1 : 1$ matching no longer supports a true $1 : 1$ matching, since lastName or firstName can be matched to one attribute while ⟨firstName, lastName⟩ is matched to another. It is also worth noting that, in the absence of any restrictions on the mapping cardinality, computing $n : 1$ correspondences may require computing 2^n pair-wise similarity measures, which is obviously intractable.

Another solution is applied if the schema matcher does not provide similarities of compound attributes. In this case, the similarity matrix will remain the same and a 2LM will be applied to this matrix, to determine whether a combination of several attributes is adequate. For example, if using some linguistic measure, name is matched with lastName at a similarity level of 0.5 and with firstName at a similarity level of 0.44, a threshold algorithm with a cutoff of 0.4 may choose both lastName and firstName to match with name. The representation and algorithmic solutions needed to deal with non-$1 : 1$ constraints in the absence of similarity measures for compound attributes is a topic for future research.

To summarize, we have shown several examples where a similarity matrix is used to model the uncertainty of schema matching. Our main observation is that while the matching technique may be complex and involved, the representation model need not be so.

3.3   REASONING WITH UNCERTAIN SCHEMA MATCHING

Having introduced a model for schema matching and the similarity matrix for capturing the uncertainty involved in attribute correspondence and schema matching, we now turn our attention to adding reasoning capabilities to manage uncertain schema matching. Such capabilities can take similarity measures, as given in similarity matrices, and turn them into a metric that can be reasoned with to create better matching results. We introduce two alternatives mechanisms for reasoning with uncertain matching, namely fuzzy set theory and probability theory. The discussion of former is taken mainly due to Gal et al. [2005a], and the latter is based on the model of Dong et al. [2007].

3.3.1   REASONING USING FUZZY SET THEORY

The formal framework for computing similarities among attribute sets is based on fuzzy relations [Klir and Yuan, 1995].

Definition 3.9   Given domains $\mathcal{D}$ and $\mathcal{D}'$, a *primitive similarity* relation is a fuzzy relation over $\mathcal{D} \times \mathcal{D}'$, denoted $\sim_\mu$, where the *matching similarity* μ (also annotated $\mu^{d,d'}$) is the membership degree of the pair $\langle d, d' \rangle$ in $\sim_\mu$.

In our model, $\mathcal{D}$ and $\mathcal{D}'$ can represent attribute domains (possible values) or attribute names, while $\mu^{d,d'}$ represents a similarity matrix entry.

A matching similarity of a primitive confidence relation is computed using some distance metric among domain members. Some desirable properties of a primitive similarity relation are as follows:

Reflexivity: $\mu^{d,d} = 1$. Reflexivity ensures that the exact matching receives the highest possible score (as in the case of two identical attributes, *e.g.*, with the same name).

Symmetry: $\mu^{d,d'} = \mu^{d',d}$. Symmetry ensures that the order in which two schemata are compared has no impact on the final outcome.

Transitivity: $\mu^{d,d''} \geq \max_{d' \in \mathcal{D}'} \min \left[\mu^{d,d'}, \mu^{d',d''} \right]$. This type of transitivity is known as the *max-min transitivity* property (*e.g.*, [Klir and Yuan, 1995], p. 130). It provides a solid foundation for the generation of fuzzy equivalence relations. As an example, one may generate α-level equivalence, which contains all pairs whose confidence measure is greater than a threshold α. While being a desirable property, transitivity is hard to achieve, and sometimes proximity relations (satisfying reflexivity and symmetry) are used instead. Such a relation may, at some α level, generate a partition of the domain, similarly to α-level equivalence. Determining the right threshold, α is a tuning problem that has been addressed by several research works in this area [Lee et al., 2007].

Example 3.10 Value matcher similarity   Consider two non-negative numeric domains $\mathcal{D} = \{0, 15, 30, 45\}$ and $\mathcal{D}' = \{0, 10, 20, 30, 40, 50\}$, both representing a fraction of an hour within which a car will be picked up. Assume that the matching similarity of elements $d \in \mathcal{D}$ and $d' \in \mathcal{D}'$ is measured according to their Euclidean distance, normalized between 0 and 1:

$$\mu^{d,d'} = 1 - \frac{|d - d'|}{\max_{d_i \in \mathcal{D}, d'_j \in \mathcal{D}'}\{|d_i - d'_j|\}} \tag{3.1}$$

Therefore, the matching similarity of 15 (in $\mathcal{D}$) and 30 (in $\mathcal{D}'$) is 0.7. This primitive similarity relation, with its associated $\mu^{d,d'}$, as defined in Equation 3.1, is reflexive (since $d - d = 0$) and symmetric (since $|d - d'| = |d' - d|$), yet nontransitive, which makes it a proximity relation. As an example, consider a third domain $\mathcal{D}'' = \{0, 30\}$. For $d = 0$ and $d'' = 30$, $\mu^{d,d''} = 0.33$, yet $\max_{d' \in \mathcal{D}'} \min\left[\mu^{d,d'}, \mu^{d',d''}\right] = 1$ (e.g., for $d' = d = 0$). □

Example 3.11 Term matcher confidence   Let $\mathcal{D}$ and $\mathcal{D}'$ be two domains whose elements are attribute names. Let $\sim_{\mu_t}$ be a primitive similarity relation over $A \times A'$, where μ_t is called the *term matching similarity measure*. The term matcher (see Example 3.3) similarity measure can be computed as follows:

$$\mu_t^{d,d'} = \frac{|d \cap d'|}{\max(|d|, |d'|)} \tag{3.2}$$

where $|d \cap d'|$ stands for the length of the longest common substring (after preprocessing such as dehyphenation). It is worth noting that, as is often common in the database literature, we let d refer to both an attribute and its name. This primitive similarity relation, with its associated $\mu_t^{d,d'}$, as defined in Equation 3.2, is reflexive since for two identical attribute names (*e.g.*, cardNum of the CardInfo and the CardInformation relations), the size of the common substring is the whole attribute name, and therefore $\mu_t = 1$. Also, it is symmetric since $|d \cap d'| = |d' \cap d|$ and $\max(|d|, |d'|) = \max(|d'|, |d|)$. However, it is nontransitive, which, again, makes it a proximity relation. As an example, consider three schemata with one attribute each, *e.g.*, firstChoice, primaryChoice, and primarySelection. While firstChoice matches primaryChoice with $\mu_t = 0.46$ and primaryChoice matches primarySelection with $\mu_t = 0.44$, matching firstChoice with primarySelection results in $\mu_t = 0$. Another method of computing attribute name similarity divides the length of the longest common substring by the length of the first (or alternatively, the second) attribute name, given by

$$\mu_t^{d,d'} = \frac{|d \cap d'|}{|d|}.$$

Clearly, such a measure is asymmetric. For example, firstChoice matches primaryChoice with $\mu_t = 0.55$, yet primaryChoice matches firstChoice with $\mu_t = 0.46$. □

By formalizing similarity measures, one can better analyze the properties of matching techniques. For example, consider the three attributes firstChoice, primaryChoice, and primarySelection, discussed in Example 3.11. This example highlights the importance of transitivity. The three attributes seem to be semantically similar, referring to some top priority option, and therefore, in the presence of three schemata, one would be interested in placing the three together in a single equivalence class. However, nontransitivity prevents the substring matching technique from achieving such a correspondence. Many of the similarity relations we have encountered are proximity relations, thus increasing the complexity of the matching process. In particular, with the introduction of a new schema, it does not suffice to perform the matching process with a single representative schema (which can be efficiently performed using simple matrix multiplication techniques) from the set of known schemata. Rather, the matching process should be performed in a pair-wise fashion with every schema in the schema set.

We next move from primitive to compound similarity relations, which are fuzzy relations as well. Compound similarity relations use similarity measures (either primitive or compound) as input to compute new similarity measures. We introduce three examples of compound similarity relations and discuss their properties.

Example 3.12   Domain similarity relation   Example 3.10 suggests a method for computing a similarity measure for value matching. We can compute the matching similarity of two such domains based on the matching similarity of their values. Let $\mathcal{D}$ and $\mathcal{D}'$ be two compound domains, whose elements are domains by themselves. Let μ_{dom} be a function, termed the *domain matching similarity measure*. Then, $\sim_{\mu_{dom}}$ is a *domain matching similarity relation*. μ_{dom} is a function of the matching similarity of every pair of elements from $\mathcal{D}$ and $\mathcal{D}'$. For example, one may compute μ_{dom} as:

$$\mu_{dom}^{\mathcal{D},\mathcal{D}'} = \min_{d \in \mathcal{D}, d' \in \mathcal{D}'} \left(\mu^{\mathcal{D},d'}, \mu^{\mathcal{D}',d} \right) \tag{3.3}$$

where for all $d' \in \mathcal{D}'$, $\mu^{\mathcal{D},d'} = \max_{d \in \mathcal{D}} \left(\mu^{d,d'} \right)$, and for all $d \in \mathcal{D}$, $\mu^{\mathcal{D}',d} = \max_{d' \in \mathcal{D}'} \left(\mu^{d,d'} \right)$. That is, each value in $\mathcal{D}$ is matched with the "best" value in $\mathcal{D}'$, and vice versa, and the strength of μ_{dom} is determined by the strength of the "weakest link." This use of min and max is in line with fuzzy logic conventions, where max is interpreted as disjunction and min is interpreted as conjunction. As a concrete example, consider $\mathcal{D}$ and $\mathcal{D}'$ of Example 3.10. Computing $\mu_{dom}^{\mathcal{D},\mathcal{D}'}$ according to Eq. 3.3 yields a matching of 0 with 0, 10 and 20 with 15, *etc.*, $\mu_{dom}^{\mathcal{D},\mathcal{D}''} = 0.9$, since each element in $\mathcal{D}'$ has a corresponding element in $\mathcal{D}$, which is at most 5 minutes apart (and $1 - \frac{5}{50} = 0.9$).

Proposition 3.13   *The domain matching similarity relation is a proximity relation.*

Proof. We shall now show that Equation 3.3 is reflexive and symmetric.

Reflexivity: From the fact that $\mathcal{D} = \mathcal{D}'$, one has that for all $d' \in \mathcal{D}$,

$$\mu^{\mathcal{D},d'} = \max_{d \in \mathcal{D}} \left(\mu^{d,d'} \right)$$
$$= \mu^{d,d}$$
$$= 1$$

Therefore,

$$\mu_{dom}^{\mathcal{D},\mathcal{D}} = \min_{d\in\mathcal{D},d'\in\mathcal{D}} \left(\mu^{\mathcal{D},d'},\mu^{\mathcal{D},d}\right) = 1$$

Symmetry: We show that $\mu_{dom}^{\mathcal{D},\mathcal{D}'} = \mu_{dom}^{\mathcal{D}',\mathcal{D}}$:

$$\begin{aligned}
\mu_{dom}^{\mathcal{D},\mathcal{D}'} &= \min_{d\in\mathcal{D},d'\in\mathcal{D}'} \left(\mu^{\mathcal{D},d'},\mu^{\mathcal{D}',d}\right) \\
&= \min_{d'\in\mathcal{D}',d\in\mathcal{D}} \left(\mu^{\mathcal{D}',d},\mu^{\mathcal{D},d'}\right) \\
&= \mu_{dom}^{\mathcal{D}',\mathcal{D}}
\end{aligned}$$

☐

In general, the computation of μ_{dom} needs to consider all non-zero similarities between elements of $\mathcal{D}$ and $\mathcal{D}'$. Therefore, the computation complexity of μ_{dom} is of $O\left(|\mathcal{D}| \times |\mathcal{D}'|\right)$, where $|\mathcal{D}|$ and $|\mathcal{D}'|$ are the cardinalities of $\mathcal{D}$ and $\mathcal{D}'$, respectively.[2] Such complexity becomes tedious for large domains. For certain special cases, however, domain similarity can be computed at a much lower cost. For example, when computing Eq. 3.3 for sorted numeric domains using Euclidean distance as the distance metric, each element in one domain needs to be matched with at most two elements in the other (using a variation of the merge-sort algorithm), reducing the overall complexity of the process to $O(|\mathcal{D}| + |\mathcal{D}'|)$. Also, if one domain has even a single value that cannot be matched with any value in the other domain (*e.g.*, as when a text value "Choose from list" is added to one of two numeric domains), then using Eq. 3.3, $\mu_{dom}^{\mathcal{D},\mathcal{D}'} = 0$. Other methods for computing domain similarity measures have been proposed in the literature. For example, Valtchev and Euzenat [1997] propose a method for computing domain similarity using a weighted bipartite graph. Such a method minimizes the dissimilarity measure, at the expense of partial matching, where there exist non-mapped values in the presence of different domain cardinalities. ☐

Example 3.14 Attribute matching similarity relation   Modica et al. [2001] determine attribute matching similarity as a combination of attribute name matching similarity (μ_t) and the matching similarity between the corresponding attribute domains, as presented in Example 3.12 (μ_{dom}). Therefore, given two attributes d, d', with domains $\mathcal{D}$ and $\mathcal{D}'$, respectively, the *attribute similarity measure* of d and d', denoted μ_{at}, is some aggregation function $\mu_{at}^{d,d'} = h_1(\mu_t^{d,d'}, \mu_{dom}^{\mathcal{D},\mathcal{D}'})$. Consider two attributes with the same name ($\mu_{at} = 1$) and corresponding domains $\{0, 15, 30, 45\}$ and $\{0, 10, 20, 30, 40, 50\}$. As shown in Example 3.12, $\mu_{dom} = 0.9$. Assuming now that $\mu_{at} = average(\mu_t, \mu_{dom})$, one has that $\mu_{at} = 0.95$. ☐

---

[2]This analysis assumes domains with a finite number of elements.

Table 3.5: Computing schema matching similarity measure

Attribute pair	μ_t	μ_{dom}	μ_{at}
lastName,name	0.5	1	0.75
firstName,name	0.44	1	0.72
arrivalDate,checkInDay	0.18	1	0.59
			0.69

Example 3.15   Schema matching similarity   Given two attribute sets, $\mathcal{A}$ and $\mathcal{A}'$, a *schema matching* F from $\mathcal{A}$ to $\mathcal{A}'$ is a set of $|\mathcal{A}|$ pairs (A, A'), such that $A \in \mathcal{A}$, $A' \in \mathcal{A}' \cup \{null\}$, and $A' = F(A)$. A matching to a null value represents no matching. $\mathcal{A} \sim_\mu \mathcal{A}'$ denotes the *schema matching similarity* of F. The *schema matching measure* μ^F is some aggregation function $\mu^F = h_2(\mu_{at}^{A,A'}|(A, A') \in F)$. A matching F is given in Table 3.5, matching relations Reservations and ReserveDetails of Example 3.1. It is worth noting that this matching is only one among many ($n!$ for $1 : 1$ matching). The table provides the computation of μ_t using the term matcher, and the computation of μ_{dom} using the min function over the pair-wise element similarity. μ_{at} is computed using the *average* function as the computation operator. Computing μ^F, by averaging over $\mu_{at}^{A,A'}$ of all the pairs (A, A') in F, yields $\mu^F = 0.69$.   □

3.3.2   REASONING USING PROBABILITY THEORY

We base our method of modeling uncertain schema matching on [Dong et al., 2007] and [Gal, 2010]. We introduce probabilistic attribute correspondences that extend the capabilities of attribute correspondences by generating multiple possible models, modeling uncertainty about which is correct, using probability theory. Such probabilities can then be combined to represent possible schema matchings, based on which query processing can be performed.

Example 3.16   For purposes of illustration, consider the case study from Example 3.1. We now describe a scenario, which we dub *semantic shift*, according to which a relation in a database, which was intended for one semantic use, changes its semantic role over the years. For example, the relation HotelCardInformation was initially designed to hold information on RoomsRUs credit cards. Over the years, the hotel chain has outsourced the management of its credit cards to an external company. As a result, the distinction between hotel credit cards and other credit cards has become vague, and new cards may be inserted in some arbitrary way into the two relations CreditCardInformation and HotelCardInformation.

Probabilistic attribute correspondences can state that R.CreditCardInfo.cardNumber matches S.CreditCardInformation.cardNumber with a probability of 0.7 and S.HotelCardInformation.clientNumber with a probability of 0.3.   □

Definition 3.17   Probabilistic Attribute Correspondence   Let S and S' be two schemata. A *probabilistic attribute correspondence* is a triple $(A, A', p_{A,A'})$, where $A \in S$ and $A' \in S'$, such that

- $p \in [0, 1]$.

- $\sum_{A'' \in S'} p_{A,A''} \leq 1$.

- $\sum_{A'' \in S} p_{A'',A'} \leq 1$.

According to Definition 3.17, a separate independent probability space is created for each attribute in S and S'. The definition allows the assignment of a positive probability to a situation in which an attribute A from schema S is not matched to any attribute in schema S'. We denote by $\bar{p}_A = 1 - \Pi_{(A,A') \in S} P(A,A')$ the probability of a non-match. Definition 3.17 is extended to probabilistic schema matching in the following way:

Definition 3.18   Probabilistic Schema Matching   A *probabilistic schema matching* is a pair (σ, p_σ), such that $\sigma \in \Sigma$ is a schema matching and $p_\sigma = \Pi_{(A,A') \in \sigma} P(A,A') \Pi_{A \in \bar{\sigma}} \bar{p}_A$.

Due to the independence of attribute probability space, the probabilities of probabilistic schema matching, as defined in Definition 3.18, are guaranteed to generate a probability space.

The intuitive interpretation of a probabilistic schema matching is that there is uncertainty about which of the matchings is the right one. There are two ways in which this uncertainty can be interpreted [Dong et al., 2007]: either a single matching should be applied to the entire set of tuples in the source relation, or a choice of a matching should be made for each of these tuples. The former is referred to as the *by-table* semantics, and the latter as the *by-tuple* semantics. The *by-tuple* semantics represents a situation in which data are gathered from multiple sources, each with a potentially different interpretation of a schema. An example that can illustrate the *by-tuple* semantics was given in Example 3.16.

We should take caution when assigning probabilities to attributes. It is common to ascribe a probabilistic interpretation to similarity measures, given the common practice of assigning similarity measures in the [0, 1] interval. Clearly, lower similarity indicates a lower perceived probability and vice versa. Yet, one should not assume a linear correlation between the two. In particular, matchers find it harder to increase a similarity measure at the extremes (very low or very high ends), something that should be captured by the assignment of probabilities. While this matter is by and large an open research topic, we will show in Section 5.5 a method for computing attribute correspondence probabilities from probabilistic schema matchings, taking into account the constraint function Γ.

3.4   ASSESSING MATCHING QUALITY

What qualifies a schema matcher to be considered "good"? Most research works offer empirical, explanatory analysis, testing schema matchers using *a posteriori* metrics. In this section, we offer an overview of the various methods for assessing matching quality, with an emphasis on matcher monotonicity.

The evaluation of schema matchings is performed with respect to an *exact matching*, based on expert opinions. *Precision* and *recall* are used for the empirical evaluation of performance. Assume that out of the $n \times n'$ attribute matchings, there are $c \le n \times n'$ correct attribute matchings, with respect to the exact matching. Also, let $t \le c$ be the number of matchings, out of the correct matchings, that were chosen by the matching algorithm, and let $f \le n \times n' - c$ be the number of incorrect attribute matchings. Then, precision is computed to be

$$P = \frac{t}{t + f}$$

and recall is computed as

$$R = \frac{t}{c}$$

Clearly, higher values of both precision and recall are desired.

Precision, recall, and their derivatives have traditionally served the research community to empirically test the performance of schema matchers. These metrics are explanatory in nature, measuring the goodness-of-fit of the heuristic to the data. The work of Do et al. [2002] provides a comparison of schema matchers using precision, recall, and two of their derivatives, namely *F-Measure* and *overall*. *F-Measure* is the harmonic mean of precision and recall:

$$FM = 2 \cdot \frac{PR}{P + R}$$

The *overall* accuracy measure evaluates post-match effort, including the amount of work needed to add undiscovered matchings and remove incorrect matchings:

$$OV = R \cdot \left(2 - \frac{1}{P}\right) = \frac{t - f}{c}$$

It is worth noting that this measure may be assigned with negative values.

Another derivative of precision and recall, dubbed *error*, was used by Modica et al. [2001] for schema matching, following Frakes and Baeza-Yates [1992]. *Error* is defined to be

$$ER = 1 - \frac{(1 + b^2)PR}{b^2 P + R}$$

where b is a tunable parameter. Intuitively, the lower the value of ER, the better the match.

Mena et al. [2000] propose the measure of information loss to quantify the uncertainty that arises in the face of possible semantic changes when translating a query across different ontologies:

$$LS = 1 - \left(\frac{1}{\gamma P^{-1} + (1 - \gamma) R^{-1}}\right)$$

where γ is a tunable parameter. It is easy to see that

$$FM = 1 - LS \quad \text{for } \gamma = 0.5$$
$$ER = LS \quad \text{for } \gamma = 1 \text{ and } b = 0$$
$$ER = 1 - FM \quad \text{for } b = 1$$

Precision and recall provide a form of pragmatic (*a posteriori*) soundness and completeness. Therefore, an exact matching is needed to measure soundness and completeness.

Schema matchings were evaluated by Benerecetti et al. [2005] using semantic soundness and completeness. This work provides a theoretical foundation that uses a complete ontology in evaluating schema matchers. The authors quote a gloomy model-theoretic argument of the philosopher H. Putnam [1981] to the effect that "two agents may agree at the conceptual level, but not at the pragmatic level." That is, while a matcher may correctly identify a relationship between two concepts, this may still not entail agreement at the instance level. With such an argument at hand, tasks such as query answerability, which is one of the tasks solved by Madhavan et al. [2002] using a formal representation language, and query rewriting, which was presented as one ultimate goal of schema matching by Gal et al. [2005b], cannot be evaluated to be sound and complete. In particular, the use of certain answers which rely heavily on an ability to agree at the conceptual level may be hindered.

Other criteria for measuring the quality of schema matchings involve lossless mapping and information capacity [Barbosa et al., 2005, Bohannon et al., 2005, Hull, 1986, Miller et al., 1993]. Using these criteria, schema matchings are measured according to their ability to reconstruct the original data.

3.4.1   THE MONOTONICITY PRINCIPLE

The monotonicity measure [Gal et al., 2005a], provides a relationship between the behavior of a given matcher and its true performance. Instead of just observing the final outcome provided by the matcher, the monotonicity principle observes the internal mechanism that leads to a matcher's decision. In that sense, it offers a deeper understanding of a matcher's capability.

We now review the basics of the monotonicity principle, based on the intuitive description first proposed by Gal [2007]. We then recall some of the main theoretical properties [Gal et al., 2005a]. We shall focus on the precision measure, where $P(\sigma)$ denotes the precision of a schema matching σ. We note that a similar analysis can be performed using precision with bounded recall, recall, F-Measure, and any other measure a designer deems suitable for assessing matcher performance.

We first create equivalence schema matching classes on 2^S. Two matchings σ' and σ'' belong to a class p if $P(\sigma') = P(\sigma'') = p$, where $p \in [0, 1]$. For each two matchings σ' and σ'', such that $P(\sigma') < P(\sigma'')$, we can compute their schema matching level of similarity, $\Omega(\sigma')$ and $\Omega(\sigma'')$.

Definition 3.19   A matching algorithm is *monotonic* if for any two matchings $\{\sigma', \sigma''\} \subseteq 2^S$, $P(\sigma') < P(\sigma'') \rightarrow \Omega(\sigma') < \Omega(\sigma'')$.

Intuitively, a matching algorithm is monotonic if it ranks all possible schema matchings according to their level of precision.

A monotonic matching algorithm easily identifies the exact matching. Let σ^* be the exact matching, then $P(\sigma^*) = 1$. For any other matching σ', $P(\sigma') < P(\sigma^*)$. Therefore, if $P(\sigma') < P(\sigma^*)$, then from monotonicity, $\Omega(\sigma') < \Omega(\sigma^*)$. All one has to do then is to devise a method for finding a matching σ^* that maximizes Ω.

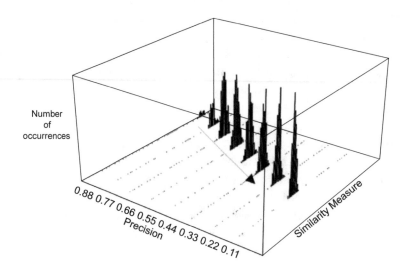

Figure 3.2: Illustration of the monotonicity principle

Figure 3.2 provides an illustration of the monotonicity principle using a matching of a simplified version of two Web forms. Both schemata have nine attributes, all of which are matched under the exact matching. Given a set of matchings, each value on the x-axis represents a class of schema matchings with a different precision. The z-axis represents the similarity measure. Finally, the y-axis stands for the number of schema matchings from a given precision class and with a given similarity measure.

Two main insights are readily noticeable from Figure 3.2. First, the similarity measures of matchings within each schema matching class form a "bell" shape, centered around a specific similarity measure. This behavior indicates a certain level of robustness, where the schema matcher assigns similar similarity measures to matchings within each class. Second, the "tails" of the bell shapes overlap. Therefore, a schema matching from a class with lower precision may receive a higher similarity measure than one from a class with higher precision. This, of course, contradicts the definition of monotonicity. However, the first observation serves as motivation for a definition of statistical monotonicity [Gal et al., 2005a], as follows:

Definition 3.20   Statistical monotonicity   Let $\Sigma = \{\sigma_1, \sigma_2, ..., \sigma_m\}$ be a set of matchings over schemata S_1 and S_2 with n_1 and n_2 attributes, respectively, and define $n = \max(n_1, n_2)$. Let $\Sigma_1, \Sigma_2, ..., \Sigma_{n+1}$ be subsets of Σ such that for all $1 \le i \le n + 1$, $\sigma \in \Sigma_i$ iff $\frac{i-1}{n} \le P(\sigma) < \frac{i}{n}$. We define M_i to be a random variable, representing the similarity measure of a randomly chosen matching from Σ_i. Σ is *statistically monotonic* if the following inequality holds for any $1 \leq i < j \leq n + 1$:

$$\bar{\Omega}(M_i) < \bar{\Omega}(M_j)$$

where $\bar{\Omega}(M)$ stands for the expected value of M.

Intuitively, a schema matching algorithm is statistically monotonic with respect to two given schemata if the expected certainty increases with precision. Statistical monotonicity can help explain certain phenomena in schema matching. For example, it can explain the lack of "industrial strength" [Bernstein et al., 2004] schema matchers and serve as a guideline as we seek better ways to use schema matchers. Also, it helps us understand why schema matcher ensembles work well (see Chapter 4). Finally, it serves as a motivation for seeking top-K matchings (see Chapter 5).

There are instances where a matcher is considered monotonic for some aggregators but not for others [Gal et al., 2005a]. Consider, for example, the min operator. Consider further two attribute sets, $\{A_1, A_2\}$ and $\{A'_1, A'_2\}$, with the following attribute correspondence similarity matrix:

	A'_1	A'_2
A_1	0.5	0.8
A_2	0.4	0.5

Let the exact matching be a matching such that A_1 is mapped with A'_1 and A_2 with A'_2. Using the average aggregator, the exact matching has a similarity of 0.5 while the best matching switches the two correspondences to be $\{\langle A_1, A'_2 \rangle, \langle A_2, A'_1 \rangle\}$ with a similarity measure of 0.6. Therefore, the set of possible matchings is non-monotonic. However, by using the min operator, the schema matching similarity of the exact matching (0.5) is higher than that of the best matching (0.4).

Another interesting observation [Gal et al., 2005a] is that the use of an average aggregator is preferred over any t-norm operator to compute matching similarity. To show this *closely related attributes* are defined to be attributes that may map well in various combinations. Any pair of attributes in a closely related attribute set has about the same similarity measure as any other pair, making it hard for a matcher to differentiate them. The paper suggests that the use of the average aggregator is more likely to yield monotonic matchings whenever attributes do not form closely related sets. It is not true, however, that any other t-norm performs better if there are closely related attribute sets.

CHAPTER 4

Schema Matcher Ensembles

If we were all determined to play the first violin we should never have an ensemble.
Therefore, respect every musician in his proper place.
– Robert Schumann

In an effort to increase the robustness of individual matchers in the face of matching uncertainty, researchers have turned to schema matcher ensembles,[1] which combine different schema
matchers that use complementary principles to judge the similarity between concepts. The idea is appealing since an ensemble of complementary matchers can potentially compensate for the weaknesses
of any given matcher in the ensemble. Indeed, several studies report on encouraging results when
using schema matcher ensembles (*e.g.*, [Do and Rahm, 2002, Embley et al., 2002, Gal et al., 2005b,
Madhavan et al., 2001, Mork et al., 2006]). Tools developed for ensemble design include eTuner
[Lee et al., 2007], LSD [Doan et al., 2001] and OntoBuilder [Marie and Gal, 2007b, 2008]. We
use the model of Chapter 3 to analyze ensembles, providing a general ensemble design framework.

4.1 THE ART OF MATCHER ENSEMBLING

A *schema matching ensemble* is a set of schema matchers. An ensemble aggregates the similarities
assigned by individual matchers to reason about the resulting aggregated ranking of alternative
matchings. Such an aggregation can be modeled in various ways. Do and Rahm [2002] represent
ensemble similarity values by a cube, aggregated into a matrix by aggregating the similarity values of
each correspondence across ensemble members. This model was studied further by Domshlak et al.
[2007], who analyzed the relationships between local and global aggregators. The former combines
the similarity measures of attribute correspondences into a schema matching similarity measure by
a single matcher. The latter combines the similarity measures of multiple matchers.

Consider a set of m schema matcher outputs $\left\{M^{(1)}, \ldots, M^{(m)}\right\}$ between two schemata S and
S'. $M_{i,j}^{(l)}$ is the degree of similarity that matcher l associates with matching the i-th attribute of S to
the j-th attribute of S'. Whenever we refer to a single matcher, we drop the superscript and refer to
the output of the matcher as M.

A *local aggregation function*, given a matching σ, and a similarity matrix M, formally given as

$$f\left(\sigma, M\right) = f\left(M_{1,\sigma(1)}, \ldots, M_{n,\sigma(n)}\right).$$

---

[1]The term *ensemble* is borrowed from He and Chang [2005] and Domshlak et al. [2007].

$M_{i,\sigma(i)}$, represents the similarity value of attribute i in S, and its matching counterpart, attribute $\sigma(i)$, in S'. $f(\sigma, M)$ is a function that aggregates the similarity measures associated with individual attribute correspondences, forming a schema matching σ. A popular choice of a local aggregator is the sum (or average) of attribute correspondence similarity measures (*e.g.*, [Do and Rahm, 2002, Gal et al., 2005b, Melnik et al., 2002]), but other local aggregators have been found appealing as well. For example, the *Dice* local aggregator, suggested by Do and Rahm [2002], is the ratio of the number of successfully matched attributes (those whose similarity measure has passed a given threshold) and the total number of attributes in both schemata. Threshold-based aggregators have been presented as well, *e.g.*, by Modica et al. [2001]. f is typically assumed to be computable in linear time in the matrix size. However, at least technically, there is no restriction on the use of more sophisticated (and possibly more computation-intense) local aggregators.

Given two schemata S and S', an ensemble of m schema matchers may utilize different local aggregators $f^{(1)}, \ldots, f^{(m)}$. Each local aggregator computes the similarity measure of a matching of a different matchers and may be tied to the specific capabilities of the matcher. For example, it may be more meaningful to apply an *average* aggregator than a min aggregator to a matcher that does not use a threshold. The m matchers produce an $m \times n \times n'$ similarity cube of $n \times n'$ similarity matrices $M^{(1)}, \ldots, M^{(m)}$. The similarity measures produced by such an ensemble of schema matchers can be aggregated, using a real-valued *global aggregation function* $F\left(f^{(1)}(\sigma, M^{(1)}), \cdots, f^{(m)}(\sigma, M^{(m)})\right)$ [Do and Rahm, 2002, Gal et al., 2005b]. $\langle \vec{f}, F \rangle$ denotes the set of local and global aggregators, respectively. The aggregated weight provided by the m matchers with $\langle \vec{f}, F \rangle$ to the matching σ is given as

$$\langle \vec{f}, F \rangle(\sigma) \equiv F\left(f^{(1)}(\sigma, M^{(1)}), \cdots, f^{(m)}(\sigma, M^{(m)})\right)$$

Many global aggregators proposed in the literature can be generalized as

$$F\left(f^{(1)}(\sigma, M^{(1)}), \cdots, f^{(m)}(\sigma, M^{(m)})\right) = \frac{\lambda}{m} \sum_{l=1}^{m} k_l f^{(l)}(\sigma, M^{(l)}), \tag{4.1}$$

where Eq. 4.1 can be interpreted as a (weighted) sum (with $\lambda = m$) or a (weighted) average (with $\lambda = 1$) of the local similarity measures, and where k_l are some arbitrary weighting parameters. It is important to note that the choice of a global aggregator is ensemble-dependent, and it is considered to be a *given* property of the ensemble.

This model represents just one possible ensemble design, a *linear parallel multiple-matcher* design model. We now extend this model in three different dimensions, to demonstrate the ensemble design space. The first two dimensions are illustrated in Table 4.1, with representative examples for each design decision in the space.

Participation dimension: Determining the participating schema matchers in an ensemble is an important tuning parameter of the matching process. In Section 4.3, we provide a method for matcher selection. Works in the literature typically construct matcher ensembles from multiple

Participation → ↓ Execution	Single	Multiple
Table 4.1: Ensemble design dimensions		
Sequential		[Duchateau et al., 2008]
Parallel	[Gal, 2006]	[Do and Rahm, 2002]

matchers. However, Example 3.8 gave an interesting twist to the notion of an ensemble: Rather than combining the input of multiple matchers, a single matcher with different settings was employed to create different "opinions." In general, in an ensemble, the first matcher provides the best possible matching between a pair of schemata. Then, each new matcher is forced to create a new matching that differs from its predecessors by at least one attribute correspondence.

Execution dimension: To date, the *parallel ensemble approach* is dominant in ensemble research. This approach involves combining the judgments of multiple matchers (a similarity cube) into a single matcher (a similarity matrix). eTuner [Lee et al., 2007], as well as others, have proposed tuning the weights of the different matchers, giving greater weight to more effective matchers. A far less common alternative is the *sequential ensemble approach*, where matchers are added to an ensemble sequentially, based on the outcomes of earlier stages. The intuitive idea behind sequential matching is to allow matchers to suggest correspondences in "regions" of the similarity matrix in which they "feel" more confident. A matcher can identify correspondences for which it is less confident and pass them on to another matcher to evaluate. Clearly, a matcher needs to be able to identify its "strong regions." An example of this line of work is that of Duchateau et al. [2008], which introduces a decision tree to combine the most appropriate matchers. The internal nodes of the tree represent attribute correspondence similarity measures, and the edges stand for conditions on the result of the similarity measure. Thus, the decision tree contains plans (*i.e.*, ordered sequences) of matchers. A leaf node accepts a Boolean value, indicating if there is a match. At any given point in the matching process, a similarity measure must satisfy the condition on an edge to access the next node. Thus, matchers that are closer to the root are executed earlier than those below them.

As for the third dimension, when designing a parallel ensemble, with either single- or multiple-matchers, aggregation can be performed linearly, as illustrated in Eq. 4.1. Algergawy [2010] proposes a non-linear aggregation, working directly with a global aggregator. Using our notation above, and given k matchers, a global aggregator will aggregate attribute correspondence similarities $\left\{ M_{i,j}^{(1)}, M_{i,j}^{(2)}, ..., M_{i,j}^{(m)} \right\}$ as follows:

$$F\left(M_{i,j}^{(1)}, M_{i,j}^{(2)}, ..., M_{i,j}^{(m)} \right) = \lambda \sum_{l=1}^{k} w_l M_{i,j}^{(l)} \pm (1 - \lambda) \sum_{p=1}^{k-1} \sum_{q=p+1}^{k} M_{i,j}^{(p)} M_{i,j}^{(q)} \qquad (4.2)$$

The first term in Eq. 4.2 combines similarity measures while ignoring interdependencies, while the second part adds the interdependencies. Similarity measures are either added or subtracted depending on the linear similarity value. The intuition behind this method of aggregation is that with greater (linear) similarity between elements, the elements are more likely to be similar, and the two parts of the equation should be added. In contrast, for low similarity, the elements are unlikely to be similar, and the second part should be subtracted. The constant λ is used to normalize the total similarity measure in the range of $[0, 1]$.

The tuning of ensemble parameters is rooted in machine learning. Machine learning has been used for schema matching in several works. For example, APFEL [Ehrig et al., 2005] determines heuristic weights and threshold levels in an ensemble using various machine learning techniques, namely decision trees (*e.g.*, C4.5), neural networks, and support vector machines. The main aspect of ensemble construction we shall tackle in the next two sections is the role of the similarity matrix. Section 4.2 demonstrates how the model of similarity measures assignment, presented in Section 3.1.2, is utilized to generate a voting mechanism among matchers. Then, in Section 4.3, we focus on the initial process of matcher selection by training a boosting algorithm over binary matrices.

4.2   2LNB: A VOTING MECHANISM FOR ENSEMBLES

In this section, we focus on one specific global aggregator, the voting mechanism. Given m binary similarity matrices, we define a voting mechanism as follows

$$F_v\left(M_{i,j}^{(1)}, M_{i,j}^{(2)}, ..., M_{i,j}^{(m)}\right) = \begin{cases} 1 & \sum_{k=1}^{m} M_{i,j}^{(k)} \geq \frac{m}{2} \\ 0 & \text{otherwise} \end{cases}$$

It is worth noting that the voting mechanism is applied to attribute correspondences, and therefore the local aggregator is not applied here. Also, since the voting mechanism requires binary similarity attributes as an input, a second line matcher that takes a similarity matrix as an input and returns a binary similarity matrix as an output should be applied before the voting mechanism kicks into action.

Marie and Gal [2007b] have shown that by analyzing the performance of first line matchers, one can successfully apply methods such as naïve Bayes to classify correspondences as either correct or incorrect. A naïve Bayes classifier is a simple probabilistic classifier based on applying Bayes' theorem with strong (naïve) independence assumptions. Although this assumption is almost always violated in practice, recent work has shown that, in some domains, like classifying text documents, the performance of this classifier is comparable to that of neural network and decision tree learning. The discussion below is mainly based on Marie and Gal [2007b].

The naïve Bayes classifier applies to learning tasks where each instance x is described by a conjunction of attribute values and where the target function $f(x)$ can take on any value from some finite set V. Consider a set of training examples $D = \{(x_1, y_1), \ldots, (x_m, y_m)\}$, where each x_i is a conjunction of attribute values and $y_i \in V$ is the true classification of x_i. Let x be a new instance, described by the tuple of attribute values $\langle a_1, a_2, \ldots, a_n \rangle$. The classifier should predict the target value for the new instance. The Bayesian approach to classify the new instance is to assign the most probable target value, v_{MAP}, given the attribute values $\langle a_1, a_2, \ldots, a_n \rangle$ that describe the instance, that is

$$v_{MAP} = argmax_{v \in V} P(v|a_1, a_2 \ldots a_n).$$

Using the Bayesian theorem, we can rewrite the previous expression as

$$v_{MAP} = argmax_{v \in V} \frac{P(v)P(a_1,a_2\ldots a_n|v)}{P(a_1,a_2\ldots a_n)} = argmax_{v \in V} P(v)P(a_1, a_2 \ldots a_n|v)$$

To estimate each $P(v)$ we must count the frequency with which each target value $v \in V$ occurs in the training set. More difficult is the estimate of $P(a_1, a_2 \ldots a_n|v)$, and to this end, the naïve Bayes approach uses the naïve assumption that the attribute values are conditionally independent given the target value:

$$P(a_1, a_2 \ldots a_n|v) = \prod_i P(a_i|v)$$

Substituting this into the last expression of v_{MAP}, we have the approach used by the naïve Bayes classifier:

$$v_{NB} = argmax_{v \in V} P(v) \prod_i P(a_i|v)$$

Recall that the values in a similarity matrix generated by a first-line matcher are assumed to form two probability distributions over [0, 1], one for incorrect attribute correspondences and another for correct correspondences (see Figure 3.1). The *second line naïve Bayes* (2LNB) heuristic attempts, given a similarity measure, to use Bayes' theorem to compute whether an attribute correspondence can be established.

Given an attribute correspondence $\left(A_i, A_j\right)$ and an ensemble of matchers $\{M^{(1)}, M^{(2)}, ..., M^{(m)}\}$, a feature vector of $\left(A_i, A_j\right)$ is defined to be $\left\langle m_{i,j}^{(1)}, m_{i,j}^{(2)}, ..., m_{i,j}^{(m)} \right\rangle$, where $m_{i,j}^{(k)}$ is the (i, j) similarity measure of $M^{(k)}$. Let $\mathcal{F}$ be an m dimension feature space. We would like to predict the most likely target value ($v = +1$ or $v = -1$), based on the observed data sample. $+1$ stands for a correct correspondence while -1 stands for an incorrect one. Formally, our target function is

$$f_c : \mathcal{F} \rightarrow \{+1, -1\} \tag{4.3}$$

The Bayesian approach to classifying a new instance (attribute correspondence in our case) is to assign the most probable target value, v_{MAP}, given the attribute similarity measure values $\left\langle m_{i,j}^{(1)}, m_{i,j}^{(2)}, ..., m_{i,j}^{(m)} \right\rangle$ that describe the instance:

$$v_{MAP} = \arg_{v \in \{+1, -1\}} \max P\left(v|m_{i,j}^{(1)}, m_{i,j}^{(2)}, ..., m_{i,j}^{(m)}\right). \tag{4.4}$$

Eq. 4.4, together with Bayes' theorem and under the simplifying assumption that the attribute similarity measures are conditionally independent given the target value, can be used to specify the target value output of the naïve Bayes classifier v_{NB} to be:

$$v_{NB} = \arg_{v \in \{+1, -1\}} \max P(v) \prod_{l=1}^{m} P\left(m_{i,j}^{(l)} | v\right) \tag{4.5}$$

$P(v)$ is estimated by counting the frequency with which each target value $v \in \{+1, -1\}$ occurs in the training dataset. $P\left(m_{i,j}^{(l)} | v\right)$, the probability of observing an attribute correspondence with similarity measure equal to $m_{i,j}^{(l)}$ given that the attribute correspondence is correct/incorrect, is taken from the estimated distribution of correct and incorrect correspondences, as suggested in Section 3.1.2.

Table 4.2: Beta parameters

Matcher	α_{pos}	β_{pos}	α_{neg}	β_{neg}
Term	0.2430	0.0831	0.2951	4.6765
Composition	0.4655	0.1466	0.8360	9.1653
Precedence	0.6071	0.1739	2.3010	13.1242
Combined	0.6406	0.2040	2.6452	16.3139

Example 4.1   To illustrate the 2LNB heuristic, consider a naïve Bayes classifier with two matchers (a bivariate instance space). Each attribute correspondence is represented by a vector of length 2, consisting of the similarity measures of the combined and composition matchers. Figure 3.1 provides an illustration of the two combined matcher distributions used by the classifier, and Table 4.2 provides the tuning parameters for the distributions. The number of negative training correspondences is $|N| = 104387$, and the number of positive training correspondences is $|P| = 1706$. Consider a new attribute correspondence with a similarity measure vector $\vec{\mu} = \langle \mu_b, \mu_p \rangle = \langle 0.5, 0.6 \rangle$ and assume that the maximum values in the combined and composition similarity matrices are $\max_{\mu_b} = 0.6$ and $\max_{\mu_p} = 0.8$, respectively. The probability of no attribute correspondence, given the vector of similarity measures $\vec{\mu} = \langle 0.5, 0.6 \rangle$, is

$$P(N|\vec{\mu}) = \frac{|N|}{|N| + |P|} \cdot P_{\alpha_{n,b}, \beta_{n,b}}(\mu_b) \cdot P_{\alpha_{n,p}, \beta_{n,p}}(\mu_p) \tag{4.6}$$

$$= \frac{104387}{104387 + 1706} \cdot 0.0097 \cdot 0.0034 = 3.2449 \times 10^{-005} \tag{4.7}$$

where $P_{\alpha_{n,b}, \beta_{n,b}}$ and $P_{\alpha_{n,p}, \beta_{n,p}}$ are the density functions of the beta distributions of the combined and composition matchers, respectively. To evaluate the probability of having an attribute correspondence, one needs to first normalize the values in $\vec{\mu}$, yielding a vector $\vec{\mu}' = \langle \mu_b', \mu_p' \rangle = \langle \frac{0.5}{0.6}, \frac{0.6}{0.8} \rangle$, followed by calculating $\frac{|P|}{|N|+|P|} \cdot P_{\alpha_{p,b}, \beta_{p,b}}(\mu_b) \cdot P_{\alpha_{p,p}, \beta_{p,p}}(\mu_p)$, yielding $P(P|\langle 0.83, 0.75 \rangle) = 0.0057$. Therefore, the naïve Bayes heuristic will determine this attribute correspondence to exist.   □

Given a pair of schemata S and S', each of cardinality n and a constant number of schema matchers m, the time complexity of running the 2LNB heuristic (not including the training phase, which can be done offline) is $O(n^2)$. m is constant, and therefore constructing a feature vector of size m costs $O(1)$ operations. The decision to classify each vector as positive or negative is made according to a simple computation, and so for each vector, its time complexity is also $O(1)$. In total, we need to perform this computation for each attribute correspondence, which means that $O(n^2)$ operations are required.

Marie and Gal [2007b] provide an empirical evaluation of the 2L naïve Bayes voting mechanism. The experiments use four matchers, namely term, composition, precedence, and combined. The combined matcher is clearly dependent on the other matchers and therefore violates the naïve Bayes heuristic assumption, which affects the experiment's outcome. Each of the four matchers is used as input to its feature vector. The 2L naïve Bayes heuristic is implemented using a Java 2 JDK version 1.5.0_09 environment, with an API to access OntoBuilder's matchers and produce the output matrices. The experiments are run on a laptop with Intel Centrino Pentium m, 1.50GHz CPU, 760MB of RAM Windows XP Home edition OS.

230 Web forms are selected from different domains, including dating and matchmaking, job hunting, Web mail, hotel reservations, news, and cosmetics sales. Schemata are derived from the Web forms using OntoBuilder and matched in pairs (115 pairs), where pairs are taken from the same domain. Exact matchings are generated manually for each pair.[2] The schemata vary in size and in the proportion of attribute correspondences in the exact matching relative to the schema size. Another relevant dimension is the size difference between matched schemata.

With four matchers and 115 pairs, 460 matrices are generated. For each matrix, the MWBG matcher (solving the Maximum Weight Bipartite Graph problem) is applied, to generate a 1 : 1 schema matching as a baseline comparison. When the first-line matchers and ensembles are combined using MWBG, the performance ranges from 0.06 to 1 in terms of precision and from 0.12 to 1 in terms of recall. Low precision and recall values indicate the weakness of the matcher with respect to a particular data set.

In addition, 100 synthetic schema pairs are generated. For each pair S and S', schema sizes are uniformly selected from the range [30, 60]. For an exact match, a set of n attribute correspondences is chosen, where n takes one of three possible values, $n_1 = \min\left(|S|, |S'|\right)$, $n_2 = 0.5n_1$, and $n_3 = 2n_1$. For n_1, a 1 : 1 cardinality constraint is enforced. n_2 represents a situation in which not all attributes can be mapped, and n_3 represents a matching that is not of 1 : 1 cardinality. Then, using the beta distributions learned from the training data for each of the four matchers, four synthetic matrices were created, one per matcher, using a beta generator class *cern.jet.random.Beta* distributed with the *colt.jar* jar file. The entries of each matrix use (α_p, β_p) and (α_n, β_n) parameters (see Table 4.2) for the beta distributions of the positive and negative similarity measures, respectively.

Precision and recall are used as the evaluation metrics. To extend precision and recall to the case of non-1 : 1 matchings, a correctness criterion is adopted, according to which any attribute

---

[2]All schemata and exact matchings are available for download from the OntoBuilder Web site, http://ie.technion.ac.il/OntoBuilder.

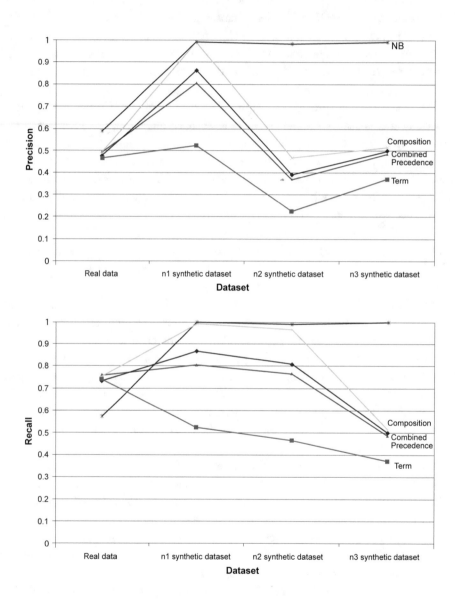

Figure 4.1: Comparative performance analysis

correspondence that belongs to the exact matching is considered to be correct, even if the complex matching is not fully captured. This method aims at compensating the matchers for the 1 : 1 cardinality enforcement.

The experiment provides a comparative analysis of the performance of the 2LNB heuristic with four heuristics that enforce a matching cardinality of 1 : 1. Figure 4.1 illustrates the results. The x axis represents the four different datasets, with precision on the y axis in Figure 4.1(top) and recall in Figure 4.1(bottom).

In terms of precision, the 2LNB heuristic outperforms all other heuristics. For the real dataset, this improvement in precision comes at the cost of recall. This disadvantage disappears in the simulated data, where the 2LNB heuristic dominates other heuristics, even for the simulated data with n_1, where the 1 : 1 cardinality constraint holds (although not enforced for the proposed heuristic). For this case, the composition heuristic comes in very close behind.

Two observations in particular may explain this behavior. First, the naïve assumption of independence does not hold in this set of experiments, since OntoBuilder heuristics are all heavily based on syntactic comparisons. Second, it is possible that the training dataset used to determine the beta distributions does not serve as a good estimator for the matchers' decision making. The latter can be improved using statistical methods for outlier elimination. For the former, a method for ensemble matcher selection is needed. Such a method is discussed next.

4.3   CONSTRUCTING ENSEMBLES

Choosing among schema matchers is far from trivial. First, the number of schema matchers is continuously growing, and this diversity by itself complicates the choice of the most appropriate tool for a given application domain. Second, as one would expect, empirical analysis shows that there is not (and may never be) a single dominant schema matcher that performs best, regardless of the data model and application domain [Gal et al., 2005a].

Most research work devoted to constructing ensembles deals with setting the relative impact of each participating matcher. For example, consider Meta-Learner [Doan et al., 2001] and OntoBuilder [Marie and Gal, 2008]. In both tools, a weighted average of the decisions taken by the matchers in an ensemble determines the matching outcome. Doan et al. [2001] sets the weights using a least-square linear regression analysis, while Marie and Gal [2008] use the boosting mechanism (to be described shortly). The literature shows a connection between boosting and logistic regression [Schapire, 2001], yet there is no evident connection to linear regression.

Research has shown that many schema matchers perform better than random choice. We argue that any (statistically) monotonic matcher is a *weak classifier* [Schapire, 1990]—a classifier that is only slightly correlated with the true classification. A *weak classifier* for binary classification problems is any algorithm that achieves a weighted empirical error on the training set which is bounded from above by $1/2 - \gamma$, $\gamma > 0$ for some distribution on the dataset (the dataset consists of weighted examples that sum to unity). In other words, it can produce a hypothesis that performs at least slightly better than random choice. The theory of weak classifiers has led to the introduction of *boosting* algorithms (*e.g.*, [Schapire, 1990]). This class of algorithms can strengthen weak classifiers to achieve arbitrarily high accuracy; they have been shown to be effective in the construction of successful classifiers. Given a set of weak classifiers, the algorithm iterates over them while re-weighting the importance of elements in the training set.

Many boosting algorithms have been proposed in the literature. Following Gal and Sagi [2010], we describe a matcher based on the AdaBoost algorithm [Freund and Schapire, 1999]. AdaBoost, presented in Section 4.3.1, is the most popular and historically most significant boosting algorithm. SMB, the boosting heuristic for schema matching, is described first, followed by a discussion of its role in selecting matchers for ensembles.

4.3.1   ADABOOST

Algorithm 1 Boosting

1: Input: $S = \{(x_1, y_1), \ldots, (x_m, y_m)\}$, and a space hypotheses $\mathcal{H}$.
2: /* $\forall 1 \leq i \leq m, x_i \in \mathcal{X}$, and $\forall 1 \leq i \leq m, y_i \in \{-1, +1\}$ */
3: /* initialization: */
4: **for all** $1 \leq i \leq m$ **do**
5:     $D_1(i) = 1/m$
6: **end for**
7: $t = 1$
8: **repeat**
9:     /* training phase: */
10:    Find the classifier $h_t : \mathcal{X} \to \{-1, +1\}, h_t \in \mathcal{H}$ that minimizes the error with respect to the distribution D_t: $h_t = \arg_{h_j} \min \varepsilon_j$.
11:    **if** $\varepsilon_t \leq 0.5$ **then**
12:        Choose $\alpha_t \in R. \, \alpha_t = \frac{1}{2} \ln \frac{1-\varepsilon_t}{\varepsilon_t}$
13:        Update $D_{t+1}(i) = \frac{D_t(i)\exp(-\alpha_t y_i h_t(x_i))}{Z_t}$ where Z_t is a normalization factor
14:        $t = t + 1$
15:    **end if**
16: **until** $t = T$ or $\varepsilon_t > 0.5$
17: /* upon arrival of a new instance: */
18: Output the final classifier: $H(x) = sign(\sum_{k=1}^{\min(t,T)} \alpha_k h_k(x))$

The AdaBoost algorithm template is given in Algorithm 1. The input to a boosting algorithm is a **set** of m examples where each example (x_i, y_i) is a pair of an instance x_i and the classification of the instance mapping, y_i. y_i typically (though not always) accepts a binary value in $\{-1, +1\}$, where -1 stands for an incorrect classification and $+1$ stands for a correct classification. Therefore, the algorithm is aimed at binary classifications. The last input element is a hypothesis space $\mathcal{H}$, a set of weak classifiers.

The algorithm works iteratively. In each iteration the input set is examined by all weak classifiers. However, from iteration to iteration the relative weight of examples changes. The common technique in the boosting literature, which is followed by Gal and Sagi [2010] as well, is to place the most weight on the examples most often misclassified in preceding iterations; this has the effect of forcing the weak classifiers to focus their attention on the "hardest" examples. Lines 4-6 of the algorithm assign an initial equal weight to all examples. Weights are updated later in line 13 (see below). An iteration counter t is set to 1 in Line 7 and increased in Line 14.

Line 10 applies weak classifiers in parallel, looking for the most accurate h_t over the weighted examples. The amount of error of each weak classifier is computed. The error measure may take many forms and in general should be proportional to the probability of incorrectly classifying an example under the current weight distribution ($\Pr_{i \sim D_t} (h_t (x_i) \neq y_i)$). At round t, the weak classifier that minimizes the error measure of the current round is chosen.

Lines 11 and 16 provide a stop condition, limiting the amount of error to no more than 50%. The stop condition also restricts the maximum number of iterations. In Line 12, the amount of change to example weights α_t is determined. Freund and Schapire [1997] show that for binary classifiers, training error can be reduced most rapidly (in a greedy way) by choosing α_t as a smoothing function over the error. Such a choice minimizes

$$Z_t = \sum_{i=1}^{m} D_t(i) e^{-\alpha_t y_i h_t(x_i)}.$$

In Line 13, the new example weights are computed for the next round ($t + 1$), using Z_t as a normalization factor.

Lines 1-16 of Algorithm 1 serve for training the algorithm weights. These weights are then used in Line 18 to classify a new instance x, by producing $H(x)$ as a weighted majority vote, where α_k is the weight of the classifier chosen in step k and $h_k(x)$ is the decision of the classifier of step k.

4.3.2   SMB: SCHEMA MATCHER BOOSTING

The boosting algorithm is trivially simple. However, Algorithm 1 is merely a shell, serving as a framework for many possible instantiations. What separates a successful instantiation from a poor one is the selection of three elements, namely the instances (x_i), the hypothesis space ($\mathcal{H}$), and the error measure (ε_t). We next show the SMB heuristic as a concrete instantiation of Algorithm 1, tailor-made to our specific problem domain of schema matching.

The example set $\{(x_i, y_i)\}$ consists of a set of attribute pairs (x_i is a pair!), comprising one attribute from each schema and belonging to the classification of the instance mapping y_i. Such a pair represents an attribute correspondence. Each instance x_i can be correct (*i.e.*, belonging to the exact matching) or incorrect. Therefore, y_i can have two possible values: ($+1$) (for a correct matching) and (-1) (for an incorrect matching). This approach can be easily extended to select multiple attributes from each schema, as long as the matcher itself can assess the similarity measure of multiple attributes. Also, to support holistic matching, examples can be designed to be sets of attributes from multiple schemata rather than a pair.

Choosing the hypothesis space is more tricky. Following our model in Section 3.1, we first note that the input to the proposed heuristic is no longer the schemata S and S', but rather a similarity matrix $M(S, S')$ (together with Γ, the constraint enforcer function). Given schemata S and S', we denote by $\mathcal{M}(S, S')$ the (possibly infinite) set of similarity matrices $M(S, S')$. The SMB heuristic is a mapping

$$\text{SMB} : \mathcal{M}(S, S')^* \times \Gamma \rightarrow M(S, S'),$$

transforming one (or more) similarity matrices into another similarity matrix. Therefore, we define the elements of the hypothesis space to be matrices. After experimenting with several variations, the most promising hypothesis space seems to be a set of second-line matchers (as defined in Section 3.1.4), of the type decision makers (whose output is a binary matrix). For example, a hypothesis h in $\mathcal{H}$ is (Term, Dominants), where the Dominants second-line matcher is applied to the outcome of the Term first-line heuristic. Among other things, Dominants serves to enforce the domain constraints, as expressed by Γ. It is worth noting that SMB is also a decision maker, and the outcome of SMB is a binary matrix.

Finally, we address the form of the error measure ε. A matcher can either determine a correct attribute matching to be incorrect (false negative), or it can determine an incorrect attribute matching to be correct (false positive). Let A_t denote the total weight of the false negative examples, C_t the total weight of the false positive examples, and B_t the total weight of the true positive examples, all in round t. Typically, one would measure error in schema matching in terms of precision and recall, translated into boosting terminology as follows:

$$P(t) = \frac{B_t}{C_t + B_t}; R(t) = \frac{B_t}{A_t + B_t} \tag{4.8}$$

These are combined using F-Measure:

$$FM(t) = \frac{2B_t}{A_t + C_t + 2B_t} \tag{4.9}$$

and therefore, a plausible error measure for the SMB heuristic is:

$$\varepsilon_t = 1 - FM(t) = 1 - \frac{2B_t}{A_t + C_t + 2B_t} = \frac{A_t + C_t}{A_t + C_t + 2B_t} \tag{4.10}$$

It is worth noting, however, that this is not the only measure possible. In particular, note that F-Measure does not take into account the matcher's success in classifying true negatives (*i.e.*, those incorrect attribute matchings which the matcher classifies as such). This is because precision and recall de-emphasize the true negative success rate. Extending precision and recall to include true negatives (using D_t as the total weight of the true negative examples) yields

$$P(t) = \frac{B_t + D_t}{A_t + B_t + D_t}$$

$$R(t) = \frac{B_t + D_t}{C_t + B_t + D_t} \tag{4.11}$$

and F-Measure

$$FM(t) = \frac{2(B_t + D_t)}{A_t + C_t + 2B_t + 2D_t} \tag{4.12}$$

which yields an error measure of

$$\varepsilon_t = 1 - FM(t) = 1 - \frac{2(B_t + D_t)}{A_t + C_t + 2B_t + 2D_t}$$

$$= \frac{A_t + C_t}{A_t + C_t + 2B_t + 2D_t} \tag{4.13}$$

Empirical evaluation suggests that Eq. 4.10 performs better than other error measures. We hypothesize that the reason for the difference in performance is that typically $|B_t| \ll |D_t|$, and with such imbalance, it is impossible to credit the matchers for their successful selection of true positives. To understand this last argument, consider two schemata of size n with an exact matching of size n (a typical example of $1:1$ matching). Therefore, there are n positive examples and $n^2 - n$ negative examples, a clear imbalance of positive and negative examples. Other efforts, using various weighing methods to balance the different sets, have yielded little improvement.

Example 4.2   This example is due to Gal and Sagi [2010]. Given the hypothesis space $\mathcal{H}$ as described above, and given a dataset of size 70, the SMB heuristic performs 5 iterations. First, it creates a dataset with equal weight for each mapping. In the first iteration, it picks (Composition, Dominants)[3], which yields the most accurate hypothesis over the initial weight distribution ($\varepsilon_1 = 0.328 \Rightarrow \alpha_1 = 0.359$). In the second iteration, the selected hypothesis is (Precedence, Intersection) with $\varepsilon_2 = 0.411$ and $\alpha_2 = 0.180$, and in the third, (Precedence, MWBG) with $\varepsilon_3 = 0.42 \Rightarrow \alpha_3 = 0.161$. The fourth hypothesis selected is (Term and Value, Intersection), with $\varepsilon_4 = 0.46$ and $\alpha_4 = 0.080$. The fifth and final selection is (Term and Value, MWBG), with $\varepsilon_5 = 0.49 \Rightarrow \alpha_5 = 0.020$. In the sixth iteration, no hypothesis performs better than 50% error, so the training phase is terminated after 5 iterations, each with strength α_t. The outcome classification rule is a linear combination of the five weak matchers with their strengths as coefficients. So, given a new attribute pair (a, a') to be considered, each of the weak matchers contributes to the final decision such that its decision is weighted by its strength. If the final decision is positive, the given attribute pair is classified as an attribute correspondence. If not, it will be classified as incorrect.   □

Let $\tilde{h}_{\max}$ be the maximum execution time of a matcher in $\mathcal{H}$ and $t_{\max}$ be the number of iterations performed by SMB. The training time of SMB is $O\left(\tilde{h}_{\max} \cdot t_{\max}\right)$. Given a new schema pair, let $n_{\max}$ be the maximum number of attributes in each schema. The cost of using SMB is $O\left(n_{\max}^2\right)$, the cost of generating the output matrix.

---

[3]Descriptions of all matchers in this example are given in Section 3.1.2.

Two comments about α_t: First, our choice of α_t limits it to be non-negative since ε_t is restricted not to exceed 0.5 (see lines 11 and 12 of Algorithm 1). This is one characteristic that differentiates SMB from the Meta-Learner of LSD, which uses a least-square linear regression on the training dataset. Second, if a hypothesis is chosen more than once during the training phase, its total weight in the decision making process is the sum of all the weights α_t with which it has been assigned.

4.3.3 ENSEMBLE CONSTRUCTION WITH SMB: EMPIRICAL ANALYSIS

Lee et al. [2007] suggest that the tuning of an ensemble involves the selection of "the right component to be executed." eTuner suggests a method for tuning "knobs" given an ensemble, but it does not provide a method for constructing it. LSD also applies the Meta-Learner to an existing ensemble. We illustrate the use of SMB in ensemble construction (rather than tuning) using an empirical setting with 30 matcher combinations (recall that the SMB hypothesis space is made of matching pairs), combining Term, Value, Composition, Precedence, Term and Value, and Combined with MWBG, SM, Dominants, Intersection, Union, and 2LNB. All algorithms were implemented using the Java 2 JDK version 1.5.0_09 environment; an API was used to access OntoBuilder's matchers and produce the output matrices. The experiments were run on a laptop with Intel Centrino Pentium m, 1.50GHz CPU, 760MB of RAM Windows XP Home edition OS.

As in the experiment setup in Section 4.2, 230 Web forms were selected from domains such as job hunting, Web mail, and hotel reservations. A schema was extracted from each Web form using OntoBuilder, and Web forms were matched in 115 pairs, where pairs were taken from the same domain; the exact matching for each pair was generated manually. The schemata varied in size from 8 to 116 attributes, with about two-thirds of the schemata having between 20 and 50 attributes. The schemata also varied in the proportion of attribute pairs in the exact matching relative to the target schema.[4] This proportion ranged from 12.5% to 100%; the proportion in about half of the schemata was more than 70%, which means that about 70% of the schema attributes could be matched. The size difference between matched schemata ranged from no difference to about 2.2 times difference in size between schemata. In about half the pairs, the difference was less than 50% of the target schema's size.

Six schema matchers (Term, Value, Composition, Precedence, Term and Value, and Combined) were run on the 115 pairs, generating 690 matrices. These matrices used the second-line matchers (MWBG, SM, Dominants, Intersection, Union, and 2LNB) to generate new matrices. 2LNB was paired only with the Combined matcher. All in all, 31 matcher pairs and 3565 pairs of real-world schemata were analyzed.

Experiments were repeated with training datasets of varying sizes. Here, we report on experiments with a training set of 60 randomly selected schema pairs and a test set of 30 schema pairs selected randomly from the remaining matrices. Each experiment was repeated three times with preprocessing as reported by Gal and Sagi [2010]. Precision and recall were used for evaluation, as discussed in Section 4.2.

---

[4]In OntoBuilder, one of the schemata is always chosen to be the target schema, the schema against which comparison is performed.

We now analyze the SMB decision making process. Given the individual performance of each matcher, one could expect that those matchers with the highest weights in the decision making of SMB will be those that perform best individually. In our case, the top four matchers in terms of precision and F-Measure are pairs in which the second-line matcher is Dominants. Figure 4.2 presents the relative matcher weights in SMB. The higher the weight, the more important the vote of a matcher regarding each attribute matching.

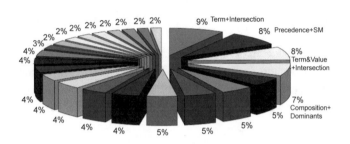

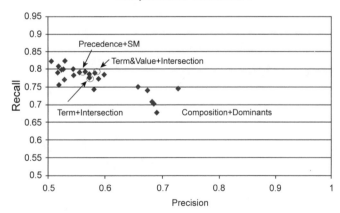

Figure 4.2: Relative matcher weights in SMB and individual performance

Only 24 of the 31 matcher pairs participated in the decision making in these experiments. SMB performs its tuning sequentially. It starts by greedily choosing those matchers that provide a correct solution to a major part of the schema matching problem. Then, it adds matchers that can provide insights for solving the harder problems. Those matchers that are left out will not be part of the ensemble.

Surprisingly, the top four matchers in Figure 4.2 (top) include only one pair with Dominants ((Composition, Dominants)). The pair (Combined, Dominants) is the leading pair in terms of precision when individual performance is considered, yet it was not even part of the SMB decision making! The most important matcher for SMB was (Term, Intersection), ranked 11th according to individual performance in terms of F-Measure and 10th in terms of precision. (Precedence, SM), ranked second for SMB, has a mediocre individual performance. Figure 4.2 (bottom) highlights the performance (on a precision vs. recall scale) of the four top matchers of SMB.

Our first observation is that the decision making of SMB is not linear in the individual performance of matchers, and therefore the SMB training process is valuable. Second, we observe that SMB seeks diversity in its decision making. It uses Term, Value (combined with Term due to its individual poor performance), Composition, and Precedence. Given these four matchers, SMB has no need for the Combined matcher, which provides a weighted average of the four. This explains the absence of (Combined, Dominants).

As a final remark, Duchateau et al. [2008] discuss a different aspect of ensemble construction. In their work, a set of matchers is built into a decision tree. Then, in run-time and based on intermediate results, the ensemble suits itself to the needs of the specific matching instance. This setting can be considered as a run-time dynamic ensemble construction as opposed to the design time construction of SMB.

CHAPTER 5

Top-K Schema Matchings

> *The quest for certainty blocks the search for meaning.*
> – Erich Fromm

Top-K schema matchings are intuitively defined as a ranked list of the best K schema matchings a matcher can generate. The formal definition, given in Section 5.1, is recursive, providing interesting insights into the behavior patterns of matchers. Top-K schema matchings play a pivotal role in managing uncertain schema matching. The effectively unlimited heterogeneity and ambiguity of data description suggests that in many cases an exact matching will not be identified as a best matching by any schema matcher. Therefore, top-K schema matchings can be used to create a search space in uncertain settings [Anaby-Tavor, 2003, Bernstein et al., 2006] and can serve in assigning probabilities in probabilistic schema matchings [Roitman et al., 2008]. They can also help improve the precision of matching results [Gal, 2006]. All in all, empirical results have shown the top-K list to be a quality set of candidates for schema matching.

We start this chapter with a formal definition of top-K schema matchings (Section 5.1). Section 5.2 provides three efficient algorithms for finding top-K schema matchings. We connect top-K schema matching with ensemble decision making in Section 5.3 and detail a heuristic that uses top-K schema matchings to improve on matcher performance in Section 5.4. We conclude with a method for using top-K schema matchings to assign probabilities to probabilistic attribute correspondences (Section 5.5).

5.1   TOP-K SCHEMA MATCHINGS: DEFINITION

We now provide a formal definition of top-K schema matching using a bipartite graph representation. For simplicity, we restrict the discussion to $1:1$ matchings. Extensions can be made by using hypergraphs, in which edges connect subsets of nodes rather than individual nodes.

Let $G = (X, Y, E)$ be an undirected bipartite graph with nodes representing attributes of two schemata and edges representing the degree of similarity between attributes. Assume a problem instance with a positive weight function $\varpi : E \to (0, 1]$ defined on edges. Given a schema matcher and a similarity matrix M, $\varpi(i, j) = M_{i,j}$. It is worth noting that G contains no edges with 0 weight. Therefore, whenever $M_{i,j} = 0$, there is no edge between attributes i and j in G. A matching σ is a subset of G's edges, $\sigma \subseteq E$. Therefore, $\sigma \subseteq E$ is equivalent to $\sigma \in \Sigma$. The weight of a matching σ is $f(\sigma, M)$, as defined in Section 4.1. Given a constraint specification Γ (see Section 3.1.3), we consider hereafter only valid schema matchings in Σ_Γ.

Top-K schema matchings can be defined recursively as follows. For $K = 1$, the K-th best matching σ_1^* is any maximum weight matching in G satisfying

$$\forall \sigma \subseteq E, f(\sigma, M) \leq f(\sigma_1^*, M).$$

Let σ_i^* denote the i-th best matching, for any $i > 1$. Then, given the best $i - 1$ matchings $\sigma_1^*, \sigma_2^*, \ldots, \sigma_{i-1}^*$, the i-th best matching σ_i^* is defined as a matching of maximum weight over matchings that differ from each of $\sigma_1^*, \sigma_2^*, \ldots, \sigma_{i-1}^*$. Therefore, given top-$K$ matchings, any matching $\sigma \subseteq E$ such that $\sigma \notin \{\sigma_1^*, \sigma_2^*, \ldots, \sigma_K^*\}$ satisfies

$$f(\sigma, M) \leq \min_{1 \leq j \leq k} f(\sigma_j^*, M) = f(\sigma_K^*, M).$$

Example 5.1   Table 3.2 (p.10) represents a similarity matrix of the running case study, illustrated graphically in Figure 5.1. Henceforth, we use attribute numbers rather than names for the sake of clarity. The exact matching (as determined by a human observer) is $\{e_{1,1}, e_{2,2}, e_{3,3}, e_{4,4}\}$, while the best matching is $\sigma^* = \{e_{1,1}, e_{2,2}, e_{3,4}, e_{4,3}\}$.   □

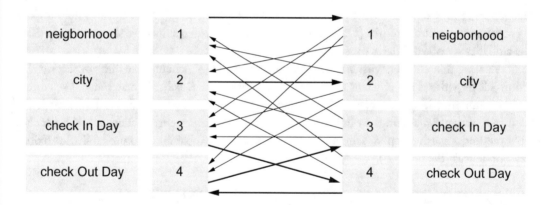

Figure 5.1: The bipartite graph of the running case study

An intuitive interpretation of top-K matchings is the following. Suppose an edge weight represents a matcher's belief in the correctness of an attribute correspondence, where a higher weight indicates greater confidence. When switching from the i-th best matching to the $(i + 1)$ best matching, the matcher is forced to give up at least one attribute correspondence, while maintaining an overall high confidence in the matching. To do so, the matcher cedes an attribute correspondence in which it is less confident. Therefore, generating top-K matchings can be seen as a process by which a matcher iteratively abandons attribute correspondences in which it is less confident.

It can be argued that top-K matchings are no different from any randomly chosen K matchings. That is, by choosing any K matchings (not necessarily the top ones), one can derive useful information on the quality of the schema matching process. We justify the decision to use top-K matchings for statistically monotonic schema matchers, discussed in Section 3.4.1, on the grounds that monotonicity ensures that the top-K matchings are sufficiently close to the exact matching.

5.2   ALGORITHMS FOR IDENTIFYING TOP-K MATCHINGS

This section introduces three algorithms for identifying top-K matchings. Given two schemata with n_1 and n_2 concepts, the first two algorithms efficiently identify the second-best matching. We then show that these algorithms do not scale for a general K. Therefore, we suggest a polynomial algorithm for identifying top-K matchings.

Given two schemata with n_1 and n_2 attributes, let $G = (X, Y, E)$ be an undirected bipartite graph with nodes representing attributes of the two schemata ($V = X \cup Y$) and edges representing the degree of similarity between attributes. We denote by A_{best} the best (complexity-wise) algorithm for finding a maximum weight matching in a bipartite graph and by $C(A_{best})$ the complexity of the algorithm A_{best}. The best known deterministic algorithm for finding maximum weight matching has a complexity of $C(A_{best}) = O(n^3)$ [Korte and Vygen, 2002], where in our case, $n = \max(n_1, n_2)$. It is worth noting that identifying the maximum weighted matching in a general graph appears to be one of the hardest combinatorial optimization problems that can be solved in polynomial time. To find the minimum weighted path for all pairs of vertices in G we shall utilize the Floyd-Warshall algorithm with a computational complexity of $O(n^3)$ (see [Cormen et al., 1990], pp. 629-634).

5.2.1   FINDING THE TOP-2 MATCHINGS USING A_{best}

Let σ_1^* be the maximum weight matching and let σ_2^* be the second-best matching in G. Observe that there exists an edge $e \in E$ such that $e \in \sigma_1^*$ yet $e \notin \sigma_2^*$. Otherwise, $\sigma_1^* \subseteq \sigma_2^*$, and since edge weights are positive, $\varpi(\sigma_2^*) > \varpi(\sigma_1^*)$, contradicting the optimality of σ_1^*. Let $G_{e'}$ denote a graph obtained from G by eliminating the edge e', for any edge $e' \in E$. Clearly, for $e \in \sigma_1^*$ given above, the matching σ_2^* is also a matching in G_e. Moreover, the matching σ_2^* is a maximum weight matching in G_e (otherwise, the existence of a matching σ in G_e of weight greater than that of σ_2^* would contradict the fact that σ_2^* is the second-best matching, since σ is also different from σ_1^*). We conclude that any maximum weight matching in G_e is a second-best matching in G since it differs from σ_1^* (in particular, it does not contain the edge e), and its weight equals that of σ_2^*, which is the second-best matching.

By the argument above, it follows that if one could correctly guess an edge $e \in \sigma_1^* \backslash \sigma_2^*$, then the second-best matching could be computed by applying A_{best} to the graph G_e. By enumerating over all possible values of e, which are all the edges of σ_1^*, we exhaustively search for σ_2^*. Let $\sigma_{\hat{e}}^*$ be a maximum weight mapping in $G_{\hat{e}}$, for each $\hat{e} \in \sigma_1^*$. Since all of these candidate solutions are different from σ_1^* and at least one of them is the second-best matching, the second-best matching can be found by picking a candidate solution of maximum weight. This leads to Algorithm 2.

Algorithm 2 Second-Best Matching

1: **for** each $e \in \sigma_1^*$ **do**
2:    $S_e \leftarrow A_{best}(G_e)$
3: **end for**
4: $e' \leftarrow \arg\max_{e \in \sigma_1^*} \omega(S_e)$
5: **return** $S_{e'}$

Table 5.1: Results of applying Algorithm 2 to the case study

Iteration	Removed edge	S_e	$\omega(S_e)$
1	e_{11}	$\{e_{13}, e_{22}, e_{31}, e_{44}\}$	0.504
2	e_{22}	$\{e_{11}, e_{23}, e_{32}, e_{44}\}$	0.463
3	e_{34}	$\{e_{11}, e_{22}, e_{33}, e_{44}\}$	0.638
4	e_{43}	$\{e_{11}, e_{22}, e_{33}, e_{44}\}$	0.638

Example 5.2   Table 5.1 presents the results of applying Algorithm 2 to the bipartite graph of Figure 5.1. The left-most column specifies the iteration number, the next column shows the edge that is removed from the graph, and the third column presents the result of running A_{best}. The right-most column provides the new weight. The algorithm returns $\{e_{11}, e_{22}, e_{33}, e_{44}\}$ with an average weight of 0.638. This is the second-best matching, which happens to be the exact matching as well. It is worth noting that not all iterations yield different matchings. For example, $\{e_{11}, e_{22}, e_{33}, e_{44}\}$ is obtained in two separate iterations, by removing either e_{34} or e_{43}. □

The correctness of the algorithm above readily follows by the preceding argument. The complexity of Algorithm 2 is $O(|V|) C(A_{best})$, which is $O(|V|^4)$ for an algorithm such as the one proposed by Korte and Vygen [2002].

5.2.2   FINDING THE TOP-2 MATCHINGS USING ALTERNATING PATHS

Given an undirected bipartite graph $G = (X, Y, E)$ with matchings σ_1 and σ_2, the edges in the set $(\sigma_1 \backslash \sigma_2) \cup (\sigma_2 \backslash \sigma_1)$ form a collection of *alternating paths* and alternating cycles in which edges of $\sigma_1 \backslash \sigma_2$ and $\sigma_2 \backslash \sigma_1$ appear in turn. We next describe a simple procedure for generating alternating paths/cycles. Consider an edge $(u, v) \in \sigma_1 \backslash \sigma_2$. Since $(u, v) \notin \sigma_2$, each of the vertices u and v is either matched to another vertex by an edge in σ_2 or not matched at all in σ_2. If u is matched in σ_2 to a vertex w, the edge (u, w) is not in σ_1 since σ_1 is a matching and there is another edge, (u, v), in σ_1 that is incident on u. Therefore, $(u, w) \in \sigma_2 \backslash \sigma_1$. A similar argument applies to v. We use the edges in $\sigma_2 \backslash \sigma_1$ incident on u and v to extend the edge (u, v) to a longer path from both ends. We continue in this vein until neither end of the extended path is matched or the ends of the path are matched to one another, forming a cycle. We discard the edges of the constructed path from $(\sigma_1 \backslash \sigma_2) \cup (\sigma_2 \backslash \sigma_1)$, and if there are still edges left we apply the described procedure to the remaining edges to construct an additional path or cycle. We continue until no edges remain.

Observe that if both σ_1 and σ_2 are matchings in which all vertices in the graph are matched, the procedure described above can only end in a cycle. As an example, consider the two matchings found in Section 5.2.1, $\sigma_1 = \{e_{11}, e_{22}, e_{34}, e_{43}\}$ and $\sigma_2 = \{e_{11}, e_{22}, e_{33}, e_{44}\}$. The edges in $\sigma_1 \setminus \sigma_2$ are e_{34} and e_{43}, and vertices 3 and 4 of the first schema are matched with vertices 4 and 3 of the second schema, respectively. Performing the procedure on $(\sigma_1 \setminus \sigma_2) \cup (\sigma_2 \setminus \sigma_1)$ yields the alternating cycle $\langle e_{43}, e_{33}, e_{34}, e_{44} \rangle$.

In this section, we describe an $O(|V|^3)$ algorithm for finding the second-best matching. We start by transforming the given graph $G(X, Y, E)$ into a complete bipartite graph with sides of equal size. This can be achieved by adding a set U of dummy vertices to the smaller side of the given graph and placing an edge of zero weight between each pair of vertices that are not connected by an edge.[1] Let $G'(X', Y', E')$ be the resulting graph.

Let σ_1^* be the maximum weight matching in G'. Assume without the loss of generality that each vertex of G' is matched in σ_1^*. Let σ be another matching in G' such that each vertex of G' is matched in σ. The edges in $(\sigma_1^* \setminus \sigma) \cup (\sigma \setminus \sigma_1^*)$ form a collection of alternating cycles. We use the latter observation to reduce the problem of finding the maximum weight matching that differs from σ_1^* to the problem of finding the minimum weight path in a graph. We define the directed graph $D(V_D, E_D)$ as follows:

$$V_D = V$$
$$E_D = E_1 \cup E_2 \text{ where}$$
$$E_1 = \{(u, v) | (u, v) \in \sigma_1^*, u \in X, v \in Y\} \text{ and}$$
$$E_2 = \{(v, u) | (u, v) \notin \sigma_1^*, u \in X, v \in Y\}.$$

We define the weight function c on the edges E_D as follows. For each $(u, v) \in E_1$, let $c(u, v) = \varpi(u, v)$. For each $(u, v) \in E_2$, let $c(u, v) = -\varpi(u, v)$.

Next, we state the algorithm for finding the second-best matching using alternating cycles. For each edge $(u, v) \in \sigma_1^*$, the algorithm constructs a minimum weight cycle in D containing the edge (u, v). Then it finds the minimum weight cycle C over all the cycles mentioned above. To compute the second-best matching in G, the algorithm starts with σ_1^* and replaces the edges from σ_1^* that appear on C by edges on C, which are not in σ_1^*.

Example 5.3   Figure 5.1 provides a pictorial illustration of $D(V_D, E_D)$. Edges of the best matching are drawn as bold solid lines. The weights were computed from Table 3.2 using c. The minimum weight paths from v_2 to u_1 for each $(u_1, v_2) \in \sigma_1^*$ are presented in Table 5.2, along with the associated cycle weights. The minimum weight cycle is $C_{43} = \{e_{43}, e_{33}, e_{34}, e_{44}\}$, which is an alternating cycle. After eliminating the edges of $C_{43} \cap \sigma_1^* = \{e_{34}, e_{43}\}$ from σ_1^* and including $C_{43} \setminus C_{43} \cap \sigma_1^* = \{e_{33}, e_{44}\}$, one identifies the second-best matching $\sigma_2^* = \{e_{11}, e_{22}, e_{33}, e_{44}\}$.   □

---

[1]Such a transformation requires a minor change in how we define edge weights to $\varpi : E \to \mathfrak{R}$.

Algorithm 3 Second-Best Matching using Alternate Cycles

1: Build the graph $D(V_D, E_D)$
2: **for** each ordered pair of vertices $i, j \in V_D$ **do**
3:     P_{ij} = minimum weight path from i to j in D (with respect to the weight function c)
4: **end for**
5: **for** each $(u, v) \in \sigma_1^*$ **do**
6:     $C_{uv} \leftarrow (u, v) \cup P_{vu}$
7: **end for**
8: $(u'v') \leftarrow \arg\min_{(u,v) \in \sigma^*} \{c(C_{uv})\}$
9: $C \leftarrow C_{u'v'}$
10: $S \leftarrow \sigma^*$
11: **for** each $(u, v) \in C \cap E_1$ **do**
12:     $S \leftarrow S \setminus \{(u, v)\}$
13: **end for**
14: **for** each $(u, v) \in C \cap E_2$ **do**
15:     $S \leftarrow S \cup \{(u, v)\}$
16: **end for**
17: **return** S

Table 5.2: Results of applying Algorithm 3 to the case study

P_{uv}	Alternating path	Associated cycle	Cycle weight
P_{11}	$\langle 1, 3, 4, 4, 3, 1 \rangle$	C_{11}	0.537
P_{22}	$\langle 2, 3, 4, 4, 3, 2 \rangle$	C_{22}	0.701
P_{43}	$\langle 4, 4, 3, 3 \rangle$	C_{34}	0.004
P_{34}	$\langle 3, 3, 4, 4 \rangle$	C_{43}	0.004

The following theorem states the correctness of the algorithm presented above.

Theorem 5.4 *The edge set S computed by Algorithm 3 is the second-best matching in G'.*

Proof. First, observe that the set S is a legal matching in G'. To see this, consider the cycle C in D computed by the algorithm. By construction of the graph D, C is an alternating cycle, *i.e.*, edges from E_1 and edges from E_2 appear on it alternately. Moreover, by construction of D, edges in E_1 correspond to the edges of the matching σ_1^*, and edges in E_2 correspond to the edges of E' that are not in σ_1^*. The set S computed by the algorithm is obtained from σ_1^* by discarding edges that correspond to edges from E_1 on C and re-matching the vertices of C using the edges of E' corresponding to the edges from E_2 on C. Since the latter set of edges are incident only on the vertices of C, so that only one edge is incident on each vertex of C, the resulting edge set is a matching in G'. Next, observe that S is different from σ_1^*, since it was obtained from σ_1^* by substituting a non-empty set of edges. Let σ_2^* be the second-best matching in G'. It remains to show that $\varpi(S) \geq \varpi(\sigma_2^*)$. Assume without the loss of generality that σ_2^* is not a proper subset of σ_1^*. (We could explicitly check the weight of each matching that is a proper subset of σ_1^* by iteratively dropping one of σ_1^*'s edges and output the matching with the greatest weight if its weight is greater than that of S.) Then we can also assume without the loss of generality that σ_2^* is a full matching (if this is not the case, we can complement σ_2^* by edges between any pair of unmatched vertices, since the graph G' is complete). Since both σ_1^* and σ_2^* are full matchings, it follows from the previous argument that the edges in $(\sigma_1^* \backslash \sigma_2^*) \cup (\sigma_2^* \backslash \sigma_1^*)$ form a collection of alternating cycles. By construction of the graph D, each cycle C_i from the collection above induces a cycle $\hat{C}_i$ in D. Clearly, the weight of the minimum cycle C computed by the algorithm does not exceed the total weight of cycles $\hat{C}_i$ with respect to the weight function c. But by definition of the function c it follows that the total weight of C_i equals $\varpi(\sigma_1^*) - \varpi(\sigma_2^*)$, and the total weight of the cycles $\hat{C}_i$ equals $\varpi(\sigma_1^*) - \varpi(\sigma_2^*)$. We conclude that

$$\varpi(\sigma_1^*) - \varpi(S) \leq \varpi(\sigma_1^*) - \varpi(\sigma_2^*)$$

yielding

$$\varpi(S) \geq \varpi(\sigma_2^*).$$

We conclude the proof by observing that according to the algorithm, there exists an edge in σ_1^* that is not S. Therefore, S differs from σ_1^* not only in dummy edges. Hence, the matching induced by S in the original graph G is also different from σ_1^*. □

Finally, we analyze the complexity of Algorithm 3. Construction of the graph D can be accomplished in $O(|V|^2)$. Finding the minimum weight paths in D between all pairs of vertices can be performed in $O(|V|^3)$ time using the Floyd-Warshall algorithm. Construction of the matching S, using the edges of the minimum weight cycle, can be completed in $O(|V|)$. We conclude that the overall complexity of the algorithm is $O(|V|^3)$.

5.2.3 FINDING THE TOP-K MATCHINGS

Algorithm 2 can be generalized in a straightforward way to solve the problem of finding the top-K matchings. We note that for each $0 \leq j \leq i - 1$, σ_i^* must contain at least one edge e_j that is not contained in σ_i^* for any natural i (the edges $e_j, 0 \leq j \leq i - 1$ need not be distinct). Let G_T denote a graph obtained from G by eliminating the edges of the subset $T = \{e_j | 0 \leq j \leq i - 1\}$. Then, using the argument presented in Section 5.2.1, we conclude that a maximum weight matching in G_T is the i-th best matching in G. Therefore, to find the i-th best matching, given $i - 1$ best matchings $\sigma_1^*, \sigma_2^*, ..., \sigma_{i-1}^*$, one could build a graph G_t for each tuple $t = (e_{1k}, e_{2j}, ..., e_{i-1l})$ (the edges in t need not be distinct) such that $e_{1k} \in \sigma_1^*, e_{2j} \in \sigma_2^*, ..., e_{i-1l} \in \sigma_{i-1}^*$, compute a maximum weight matching M_t in G_t, and choose a matching having the maximum weight over all the constructed matchings. To find top-K matchings, one could apply the described procedure for each $i = 1, 2, ..., K$.

Unfortunately, the algorithm described above has an exponential running time. This follows from the fact that the number of such tuples of E of size K grows exponentially with K, leading to an exponential number of invocations of the algorithm A_{best} for finding the maximum weight matching. Yet, as we show next, the ideas described above can be used to design a polynomial time algorithm to find top-K matchings.

We apply the dynamic programming technique to make better use of the information obtained from earlier invocations of A_{best} and reduce the number of invocations of A_{best} to be polynomial. Our algorithm is based on solutions to the assignment ranking problem, which involves the enumeration of K assignments with least cost. The first algorithm of $O\left(K\,|V|^4\right)$ for ranking assignments was suggested by Murty [1968], where $|V|$ is the number of nodes in the assignment graph. Hamacher and Queyranne [1985/6] proposed an alternative general algorithm for ranking solutions of combinatorial problems. This algorithm was later specialized for bipartite matchings [Chegireddy and Hamacher, 1987] in $O\left(K\,|V|^3\right)$, using flow networks. Pascoal et al. [2003] presented another $O\left(K\,|V|^3\right)$, using a specific order of analyzing assignments.

Our algorithm constructs a tree T of invocations of A_{best}. Each node u in T is associated with some matching $\sigma(u)$ in G and contains specifications of a subset $S_i(u) \subseteq E$ of edges that must be included in $\sigma(u)$ and a subset $S_e(u) \subseteq E$ of edges that must be excluded from $\sigma(u)$. A maximum weight matching $\sigma(u)$ satisfying these specifications is constructed by the algorithm as follows. The algorithm first discards the edges of S_e from G. Then, for each edge $(v_1, v_2) \in S_i$, the algorithm discards from G edges adjacent either to v_1 or to v_2. Let $G'(u)$ be the resulting graph. The algorithm invokes A_{best} to compute the maximum weight matching $\sigma'(u)$ in $G'(u)$. Finally, $\sigma(u)$ is obtained from $\sigma'(u)$ by adding edges of $S_i(u)$. The weight of the matching $\sigma(u)$ is referred to as the weight of the node u and denoted $\varpi(u)$.

The algorithm starts by constructing the root r of T with $S_e(r) = \emptyset$ and $S_i(r) = \emptyset$. The root corresponds to the invocation of A_{best} in the original graph G, yielding the maximum weight matching $\sigma(r) = \sigma_1^*$. Following the notation defined above, $\varpi(r) = \varpi\left(\sigma_1^*\right)$. The algorithm expands the tree iteratively. At each iteration, the algorithm first chooses a leaf to expand. For this purpose, the algorithm picks the maximum weight leaf over all the leaves of T at the current iteration. Let w be the leaf picked by the algorithm and let $\sigma(w)$ be the matching computed by the algorithm for the leaf w. Recall that $S_i(w) \subseteq \sigma(w)$, $S_e(w) \cap \sigma(w) = \emptyset$ and let $D(w) = \sigma(w) \backslash S_i(w)$ and $e_1, e_2, ..., e_t$ be the edges of $D(w)$. The algorithm builds t children of w in T, denoted $w_1, w_2, ..., w_t$. For each child w_j, where $j = 1, ..., t$, we define

$$S_e\left(w_j\right) = S_e(w) \cup \{e_j\}$$
$$S_i\left(w_j\right) = S_i(w) \cup \bigcup_{l=1}^{j-1} \{e_l\}.$$

Observe that the definition above ensures that the matchings $\sigma(w_j)$, $j = 1, ..., t$ are pairwise different.

At each iteration i, the algorithm outputs the matching $\sigma(w_j)$ corresponding to the maximum weight leaf w as the i-th best matching. The algorithm stops after K iterations.

Algorithm 4 K Best Matchings

1: KBest(G, k):
2: BuildRoot(T, r)
3: $S_i(r) \leftarrow \emptyset$
4: $S_e(r) \leftarrow \emptyset$
5: $\sigma(r) \leftarrow$ ComputeMatching($G, S_i(r), S_e(r)$)
6: **for** $i = 1$ to k **do**
7:     $w \leftarrow \arg\max_{u \ leaf \ in \ T} \varpi(u)$
8:     **return** $\sigma(w)$
9:     **if** $i - k$ **then**
10:         stop
11:     **end if**
12:     $D(w) \leftarrow \sigma(w) \backslash S_i(w) = \{e_1, e_2, \ldots, e_t\}$
13:     **if** $D(w) = \emptyset$ **then**
14:         $\varpi(w) \leftarrow 0$
15:     **end if**
16:     **for** $j = 1$ to t **do**
17:         BuildChild(T, w, w_j)
18:         $S_e(w_j) = S_e(w) \cup \{e_j\}$
19:         $S_i(w_j) = S_i(w) \cup \bigcup_{l=1}^{j-1} \{e_l\}$
20:         $\sigma(w_j) \leftarrow$ ComputeMatching($G, S_i(w_j), S_e(w_j)$)
21:     **end for**
22: **end for**

The pseudocode of the algorithm is given in Algorithm 4 and the procedure of computing a matching is given in Algorithm 5. The algorithm uses procedure *BuildRoot(T,r)*, which constructs a tree T containing the single node r, and procedure *BuildChild(T,a,b)*, which adds a child b to the node a in the tree T.

It is worth noting that if $D(w) = \emptyset$, then there are no edges to consider for elimination when expanding the tree. Therefore, if w is found to be the i-th best matching and $i < k$, then the $i + 1$-th best matching should be a different node than w, yet from the same frontier. This is done by setting the weight of w to be 0.

Example 5.5 The tree built by applying Algorithm 4 to the example, with $K = 3$, is given in Figure 5.2. The root of the tree represents the best matching (since before the first iteration the *ComputeMatching* procedure runs on the original graph). At each subtree, we consider for elimination the edges in $D(w)$ (w being the root of the subtree). Node w_1 is the best matching among matchings that exclude e_{11}. Similarly, in the first iteration for $j = 2$, we compute $\sigma(w_2)$, which is the best

---

Algorithm 5 Compute a Matching

1: ComputeMatching($G(V, E), S_i, S_e$):
2: $E' \leftarrow E \backslash S_e$
3: **for** each $(u, v) \in S_i$ **do**
4:      **for** each e adjacent on u or v in G **do**
5:          $E' \leftarrow E' \backslash \{e\}$
6:      **end for**
7: **end for**
8: $\sigma \leftarrow A_{best}(G'(V, E'))$
9: $\sigma \leftarrow \sigma \cup S_i$
10: **return** σ

---

matching among the matchings that exclude e_{22} yet include e_{11}. After expanding all the root's children to the desired level, we choose the leaf with maximum weight. In this case, it is w_3 with weight 0.3674. $\sigma(w_3) = \{e_{11}, e_{22}, e_{33}, e_{44}\}$ is the second-best matching (the same result as obtained by algorithms 2 and 3). In the next iteration, we expand w_3. Consider, for example, w_{31}. $S_e(w_{31}) = \{e_{34}, e_{33}\}$. These two edges are excluded from $\sigma(w_{31})$. e_{34} stems from σ_1^* while e_{33} stems from σ_2^*. The third iteration starts after all of w_3's children are found. The node with the maximum weight among all the nodes in the tree's frontier is now w_4. Therefore, $\sigma(w_4) = \{e11, e22, e34\}$ is chosen to be σ_3^*, the third-best matching. □

Next, we prove the correctness of the algorithm.

Lemma 5.6   *Procedure ComputeMatching($G(V, E), S_i, S_e$) constructs a maximum weight matching over matchings in G that contain edges from S_i and do not contain edges from S_e.*

Proof. The correctness of the lemma follows immediately by observing that any matching in G that contains S_i and does not contain any edge from S_e is also a matching in the graph $G'(V, E')$, constructed by the procedure ComputeMatching($G(V, E), S_i, S_e$). □

Lemma 5.7   *Let w be a node in the tree T constructed by Algorithm 4 and let $w_1, ..., w_t$ be all the children of w in T. Then any matching satisfying constraints implied by $S_i(w), S_e(w)$, and different from $\sigma(w)$ must satisfy constraints implied by $S_i(w_j), S_e(w_j)$ for some $j, 1 \leq j \leq t$.*

Proof. The correctness of the lemma follows by the definition of $S_i(w_j), S_e(w_j), 1 \leq j \leq k$ and by the fact that for any matching σ different from $\sigma(w)$ there exists an edge $e \in \sigma(w)$ such that $e \notin \sigma$. □

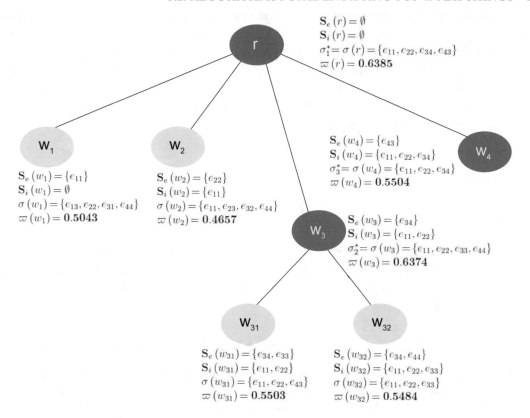

$$S_e(r) = \emptyset$$
$$S_i(r) = \emptyset$$
$$\sigma_1^* = \sigma(r) = \{e_{11}, e_{22}, e_{34}, e_{43}\}$$
$$\varpi(r) = \mathbf{0.6385}$$

$$S_e(w_4) = \{e_{43}\}$$
$$S_i(w_4) = \{e_{11}, e_{22}, e_{34}\}$$
$$\sigma_3^* = \sigma(w_4) = \{e_{11}, e_{22}, e_{34}\}$$
$$\varpi(w_4) = \mathbf{0.5504}$$

$$S_e(w_1) = \{e_{11}\}$$
$$S_i(w_1) = \emptyset$$
$$\sigma(w_1) = \{e_{13}, e_{22}, e_{31}, e_{44}\}$$
$$\varpi(w_1) = \mathbf{0.5043}$$

$$S_e(w_2) = \{e_{22}\}$$
$$S_i(w_2) = \{e_{11}\}$$
$$\sigma(w_2) = \{e_{11}, e_{23}, e_{32}, e_{44}\}$$
$$\varpi(w_2) = \mathbf{0.4657}$$

$$S_e(w_3) = \{e_{34}\}$$
$$S_i(w_3) = \{e_{11}, e_{22}\}$$
$$\sigma_2^* = \sigma(w_3) = \{e_{11}, e_{22}, e_{33}, e_{44}\}$$
$$\varpi(w_3) = \mathbf{0.6374}$$

$$S_e(w_{31}) = \{e_{34}, e_{33}\}$$
$$S_i(w_{31}) = \{e_{11}, e_{22}\}$$
$$\sigma(w_{31}) = \{e_{11}, e_{22}, e_{43}\}$$
$$\varpi(w_{31}) = \mathbf{0.5503}$$

$$S_e(w_{32}) = \{e_{34}, e_{44}\}$$
$$S_i(w_{32}) = \{e_{11}, e_{22}, e_{33}\}$$
$$\sigma(w_{32}) = \{e_{11}, e_{22}, e_{33}\}$$
$$\varpi(w_{32}) = \mathbf{0.5484}$$

Figure 5.2: An illustration showing the execution of Algorithm 4

In what follows, we refer to each iteration of the outer loop (lines 6-22) in Algorithm 4 as *an iteration.* Let T_i denote the tree T constructed by the end of iteration i of the algorithm, and let M_i be the matching which the algorithm outputs at the beginning of iteration i.

Lemma 5.8   *Let $u_1, u_2, ..., u_{n_i}$ be the leaves of T_i, $1 \le i \le k$. Then any matching in G that is different from each of $\sigma_1^*, \sigma_2^* ..., \sigma_i^*$ must satisfy the constraints implied by $S_i(u_j)$ and $S_e(u_j)$ for some j, $1 \le j \le n_i$.*

Proof. We prove the lemma by induction on i. To prove the basis of the induction for $i = 1$, we observe that by the end of the first iteration the only leaves of T_1 are the children of r. Moreover, $S_i(r) = S_e(r) = \emptyset$. Therefore, the correctness of the induction's basis follows Lemma 5.7. For the induction step, we assume that the statement of the lemma holds by the end of iteration i, and prove that it still holds by the end of iteration $i + 1$. Let $u_1, u_2, ..., u_{n_i}$ be leaves of T_i and let $x_1, ..., x_{n_{i+1}}$ be leaves of T_{i+1}. By the algorithm, leaves of T_{i+1} are obtained from leaves of T_i by removing some leaf u_j and adding its children, constructed by the algorithm at iteration $i + 1$. By the induction hypothesis, any matching different from $\sigma_1^*, \sigma_2^* ..., \sigma_i^*$ must satisfy constraints implied by $S_i(u_l)$ and $S_e(u_l)$ for some l, $1 \leq l \leq n_i$. Therefore, any matching σ different from $\sigma_1^*, \sigma_2^* ..., \sigma_i^*$ must satisfy one of the latter constraints. In addition, if σ satisfies constraints implied by $S_i(u_j)$ and $S_e(u_j)$, which correspond to the leaf expanded at the i-th iteration, then by Lemma 5.7 it must also satisfy constraints implied by one of the children of u_j. We get that σ satisfies constraints $S_i(x_p)$ and $S_e(x_p)$ for some p, $1 \leq p \leq n_{i+1}$, proving the induction step. □

Theorem 5.9 *Algorithm 4 generates top-K matchings in G.*

Proof. The correctness of the theorem follows by Lemma 5.6 and Lemma 5.8. □

Finally, we analyze the complexity of Algorithm 4. The algorithm performs k iterations. Each iteration requires invocation of the algorithm A_{best} $O(|V|)$ times and finding the maximum matching on the tree frontier in $O(log(k))$. We conclude that the overall complexity of the algorithm is $O(klog(k) + k|V|C(A_{best}))$.

5.3 EXTENDING TOP-*K* IDENTIFICATION TO ENSEMBLES

In this section, we present several algorithms for connecting the ensemble approach of Chapter 4 and the top-*K* approach, increasing the robustness of the schema matching process by enjoying the best of both worlds. Domshlak et al. [2007] introduced a generic computational framework, *schema metamatching*, for computing the top-*K* prefix of a "consensus" ranking of alternative matchings between two schemata, given the graded valid schema matchings provided individually by the members of an ensemble. Their starting point is based on rank aggregation techniques developed in the areas of Web search and database middleware [Dwork et al., 2001, Fagin et al., 2003]. They show that the Threshold algorithm, originally proposed in the context of database middleware by Fagin et al. [2003], can be applied to identify a consensus top-*K* schema matchings almost as is. Unfortunately, computing top-*K* schema matchings using the Threshold algorithm may require time exponential in the size of the matched schemata. Therefore, techniques that exploit the specifics of the schema matching problem were developed to create a simple algorithm, the Matrix-Direct algorithm, whose time complexity is polynomial in the size of the matched schemata and the required *K*. The Matrix-Direct algorithm can be applied for a certain broad class of problems, and it was extended to the Matrix-Direct-with-Bounding algorithm, which draws upon both the Matrix-Direct and Threshold algorithms to address matching scenarios where the Matrix-Direct algorithm is inapplicable. The Threshold and Matrix-Direct-with-Bounding algorithms were shown to be (complexity-wise) mutually undominated—that is, there exist problem instances in which one algorithm performs dramatically better than the other. This was resolved by introduction of the CrossThreshold algorithm, a hybrid version of these two algorithms, based on their in-parallel, *mutually-enhancing* execution.

Empirical analysis shows this hybrid algorithm to be effective, dominating both the Threshold and Matrix-Direct-with-Bounding algorithms.

We shall use the notation introduced in Section 4.1. For a schema matcher with a similarity matrix M, we define an ordering $\succeq_M$ over Σ_Γ. For schema matchings $\sigma, \sigma' \in \Sigma_\Gamma, \sigma \succeq_M \sigma'$ means that the similarity measure of σ is as high as that of σ'. It is worth noting that such an ordering may be given either implicitly or explicitly. The ordering $\succeq_M$ on Σ_Γ is therefore

$$\sigma \succeq_M \sigma' \quad \Leftrightarrow \quad f(\sigma, M) \geq f(\sigma', M)$$

for each $\sigma, \sigma' \in \Sigma_\Gamma$.

Given an ensemble of m schema matchers, utilizing (possibly different) local aggregators $f^{(1)}, \ldots, f^{(m)}$, respectively, a "consensus" ordering $\succeq$ over Σ_Γ from the individual orderings $\succeq_1, \ldots, \succeq_m$ is performed using the global aggregator F:

$$\sigma \succeq \sigma' \quad \Leftrightarrow \quad \langle \vec{f}, F \rangle(\sigma) \geq \langle \vec{f}, F \rangle(\sigma')$$

for each $\sigma, \sigma' \in \Sigma_\Gamma$.

The *schema metamatching* problem is that of generating top-K valid matchings between two schemata S and S' with respect to an ensemble of schema matchers, their respective local aggregators $f^{(1)}, \ldots, f^{(m)}$, and the ensemble's global aggregator F. Formally, given S, S', Γ, and $K \geq 1$, our task is to generate $\{\sigma_1^*, \sigma_2^* \ldots, \sigma_K^*\} \subseteq \Sigma_\Gamma$, where the i-th best matching σ_i^* is inductively defined as:

$$\sigma_i^* = \arg \max_\sigma \left\{ \langle \vec{f}, F \rangle(\sigma) \mid \sigma \in \Sigma_\Gamma \setminus \{\sigma_1^*, \sigma_2^* \ldots, \sigma_{i-1}^*\} \right\}. \tag{5.1}$$

We shall present two of the four algorithms presented by Domshlak et al. [2007]. The Matrix-Direct algorithm, an extension of the COMA approach, will be presented in Section 5.3.1. Section 5.3.2 discusses the extension of Matrix-Direct to Matrix-Direct-with-Bounding.

5.3.1   THE MATRIX-DIRECT ALGORITHM

Domshlak et al. [2007] defined a class of aggregators $\langle \vec{f}, F \rangle$ for which the order of computation can be exchanged freely, yielding possibly improved performance. As an example, consider the following local and global aggregators

$$\forall l \in \{1, \ldots, m\} : f^{(l)}(\sigma, M^{(l)}) = \sum_{i=1}^{n} M_{i,\sigma(i)}^{(l)}$$

$$\langle \vec{f}, F \rangle(\sigma) = \sum_{l=1}^{m} k_l f^{(l)}(\sigma, M^{(l)}). \tag{5.2}$$

Observe that the summations in Eq. 5.2 can be distributed, resulting in

$$\langle f, F \rangle(\sigma) = \sum_{i=1}^{n} \sum_{l=1}^{m} k_l M_{i,\sigma(i)}^{(l)},$$

where the vector notation $\vec{f}$ is replaced by f to explicitly highlight the uniqueness of the local aggregator in this case. That is, if the local aggregator f and global aggregator F happen to be as in Eq. 5.2, then using F for *local* similarity measure aggregation and f for *global* similarity measure aggregation will be *equivalent* to using f and F in their original roles. In other words, in the case of Eq. 5.2, we have $\langle f, F \rangle (\sigma) = \langle F, f \rangle (\sigma)$ for any matching σ between any pair of schemata S and S'. The special case of Eq. 5.2 can be generalized as follows:

Definition 5.10   Given a set of similarity matrices $M^{(1)}, \ldots, M^{(m)}$ over a pair of schemata S, S', and a pair of local and global aggregators f and F, we say that f and F *commute on* $M^{(1)}, \ldots, M^{(m)}$ if and only if, for every matching σ between S and S', we have:

$$\langle f, F \rangle (\sigma) = \langle F, f \rangle (\sigma). \tag{5.3}$$

Likewise, if f and F commute on all possible sets of similarity matrices, then we say that f and F are *strongly commutative*.

For instance, the aggregators f and F, as in Eq. 5.2, are strongly commutative using Definition 5.10. To illustrate commutativity in the absence of strong commutativity, consider a pair of aggregators corresponding to min and *product*. While these two aggregators are clearly not strongly commutative, they do commute, for instance, on any set of binary similarity matrices.

Algorithm 6 The Matrix-Direct (MD) Algorithm.

1: Given m matchers, construct a new schema matcher with
2:   (a) similarity matrix M^* such that
3:     for $1 \leq i \leq n, 1 \leq j \leq n', M^*_{i,j} = F(M^{(1)}_{i,j}, \cdots, M^{(m)}_{i,j})$
4:   (b) local aggregator $f(\sigma, M^*)$
5: Using Algorithm 4, generate top-K valid matchings with respect to the new matcher.

The commutativity between the local and global aggregators leads to an extremely efficient algorithm for schema metamatching. Algorithm 6 presents the pseudo-code for the Matrix-Direct algorithm (or MD, for short), generalizing the applicability of the composite method of COMA [Do and Rahm, 2002] to any schema metamatching problem in which all the matchers use the same local aggregator, and the local and global aggregators commute on the given set of similarity matrices. The correctness and time complexity of the MD algorithm are stated by Theorem 5.11 below.

Theorem 5.11   *Given a set of schema matchers and a pair of local and global aggregators $\langle f, F \rangle$, let M^* be a matrix defined as $M^*_{i,j} = F(M^{(1)}_{i,j}, \cdots, M^{(m)}_{i,j})$, for all $1 \leq i \leq n, 1 \leq j \leq n'$. If f and F commute on the similarity matrices $M^{(1)}, \ldots, M^{(m)}$, then the MD algorithm correctly finds top-K valid matchings with respect to the aggregated ranking in time $O(\max(n, n')^2 m + \Phi)$, where Φ is the time complexity of Algorithm 4 over M^*.*

Proof. The correctness is immediately discernible from the construction of the MD algorithm and Definition 5.10. As F is assumed to be computable in time linear in the number of F's parameters, generating M^* takes time $O(\max(n, n')^2 m)$. Thus, the overall complexity of the MD algorithm is $O(\max(n, n')^2 m + \Phi)$. $\square$

5.3.2   MATRIX-DIRECT ALGORITHM WITH BOUNDING

We now extend the MD algorithm to deal with non-commutative functions.

Definition 5.12   Consider a set of similarity matrices $M^{(1)}, \ldots, M^{(m)}$ over a pair of schemas S, S', and two sets of local and global aggregators $\langle \vec{f}, F \rangle$ and $\langle \vec{f'}, F' \rangle$. We say that $\langle \vec{f'}, F' \rangle$ *dominates* $\langle \vec{f}, F \rangle$ *on* $M^{(1)}, \ldots, M^{(m)}$ (denoted as $\langle \vec{f'}, F' \rangle \succ \langle \vec{f}, F \rangle$) if, for every matching σ from S to S', we have:

$$\langle \vec{f'}, F' \rangle(\sigma) \geq \langle \vec{f}, F \rangle(\sigma). \tag{5.4}$$

Likewise, if Eq. 5.4 holds for all possible sets of similarity matrices, then we say that $\langle \vec{f'}, F' \rangle$ *strongly dominates* $\langle \vec{f}, F \rangle$.

Consider a schema metamatching problem defined by a set of similarity matrices $M^{(1)}, \ldots, M^{(m)}$ and a set of local and global aggregators $\langle \vec{f}, F \rangle$ that *do not* commute on $M^{(1)}, \ldots, M^{(m)}$. Suppose that there exists a pair of functions $\langle h, H \rangle$ that (i) *do* commute on $M^{(1)}, \ldots, M^{(m)}$, and (ii) dominate $\langle \vec{f}, F \rangle$ on these matrices. Corollary 5.13, which follows immediately from the definition of the MD algorithm, defines a simple property of this algorithm that provides some intuition for the subsequent construction steps.

Corollary 5.13   *Given a set of schema matchers and a pair of local and global aggregators $\langle h, H \rangle$ commuting on $M^{(1)}, \ldots, M^{(m)}$, the top-K result of the MD algorithm with respect to $\langle h, H \rangle$ is a correct top-K aggregation with respect to any set of local and global aggregators $\langle \vec{f}, F \rangle$, such that both $\langle h, H \rangle \succ \langle \vec{f}, F \rangle$ and $\langle \vec{f}, F \rangle \succ \langle h, H \rangle$ hold on $M^{(1)}, \ldots, M^{(m)}$.*

In general, nothing prevents Corollary 5.13 from being realized. To illustrate, consider the following set of four real-valued functions: $f(x) = x^2$, $F(x) = x/2$, $h(x) = x^2/2$, $H(x) = x$. While f and F do not commute on reals ($F(f(x)) = x^2/2$ and $f(F(x)) = x^2/4$), the functions h and H are strongly commutative ($H(h(x)) = h(H(x)) = x^2/2$), and we have $H(h(x)) = F(f(x))$. Corollary 5.13 provides us with some useful intuitions. Consider a schema metamatching problem defined by a set of similarity matrices $M^{(1)}, \ldots, M^{(m)}$ and local and global aggregators $\langle \vec{f}, F \rangle$ that *do not* commute on $M^{(1)}, \ldots, M^{(m)}$. It is worth noting that we allow different matchers to use different local aggregators and in such cases, $\langle \vec{f}, F \rangle$ is (trivially) defined not to commute on $M^{(1)}, \ldots, M^{(m)}$. Suppose there exists a pair of functions $\langle h, H \rangle$ that *do* commute on $M^{(1)}, \ldots, M^{(m)}$ and dominate

$\langle \vec{f}, F \rangle$ on these matrices, yet are not dominated by $\langle \vec{f}, F \rangle$. For instance, let F be a weighted sum as in Eq. 5.2, and f be defined as:

$$f^{(i)}(\sigma, M) = \begin{cases} \sum_{j=1}^{n} M_{j,\sigma(j)}, & \sum_{j=1}^{n} M_{j,\sigma(j)} > t_i \\ 0, & \text{otherwise} \end{cases}, \tag{5.5}$$

where $t_i > 0$ is some predefined constant threshold. The intuition behind Eq. 5.5 is that matchers which can no longer provide matchings with sufficient similarity (set as the threshold t_i) "quit" by nullifying all further matchings. Another example, reflecting one of the settings used in schema matching (*e.g.*, [Bilke and Naumann, 2005, Modica et al., 2001]), is:

$$f^{(i)}(\sigma, M) = \sum_{j=1}^{n} \left(M_{j,\sigma(j)} \cdot \delta \left(M_{j,\sigma(j)} > t_j \right) \right) \tag{5.6}$$

where δ is the Kronecker discrete delta function. According to Eq. 5.6, individual pair-wise attribute matchings that do not pass a predefined, matcher-specific threshold are nullified. In both cases, it is not hard to verify that $\vec{f}$ and F do not commute (in all but trivial cases of effectively redundant thresholds.) On the other hand, functions h and H standing for simple sum and weighted sum (as in Eq. 5.2) are (strongly) commutative, and we have $\langle \vec{f}, F \rangle \prec \langle h, H \rangle$ for both Eqs. 5.5 and 5.6. For such cases, we now present the Matrix-Direct-with-Bounding algorithm (or MDB, for short).

The MDB algorithm pseudocode is given as Algorithm 7. Consider a schema metamatching problem with aggregators $\langle \vec{f}, F \rangle$ that do not commute on $M^{(1)}, \ldots, M^{(m)}$. The basic idea behind the MDB algorithm is to use a pair of functions $\langle h, H \rangle$ (that both dominate $\langle \vec{f}, F \rangle$ and commute on $M^{(1)}, \ldots, M^{(m)}$) as an upper bound for the "inconvenient" $\langle \vec{f}, F \rangle$ of our actual interest. The MDB algorithm behaves similarly to the MD algorithm if the latter is given with the aggregators $\langle h, H \rangle$. However, instead of reporting immediately on the generated matchings σ, the MDB algorithm uses the decreasing aggregated weights of $\langle h, H \rangle(\sigma)$ to update the value of a threshold τ_{MDB}. It is worth noting that, due to commutativity of h and H (either strong or just with respect to $M^{(1)}, \ldots, M^{(m)}$), we have $\tau_{MDB} = \langle H, h \rangle(\sigma) = \langle h, H \rangle(\sigma)$. The threshold τ_{MDB} is used to judge our progress with respect to the weights $\langle \vec{f}, F \rangle$ that really matter. Theorem 5.14 shows that the MDB algorithm is correct for any such upper bound $\langle h, H \rangle$.

Theorem 5.14   *Consider a set of m schema matchers with $\langle \vec{f}, F \rangle$ being their local and global aggregators. Given a function pair $\langle h, H \rangle$ that both commute and dominate $\langle \vec{f}, F \rangle$ on $M^{(1)}, \ldots, M^{(m)}$, the MDB algorithm correctly finds top-K valid matchings with respect to $\langle \vec{f}, F \rangle$.*

Proof. Let Y be as in step 16 of the MDB algorithm. We need only show that every matching $\sigma \in Y$ has at least as high weight according to $\langle \vec{f}, F \rangle$ as every matching $\sigma' \notin Y$. By the definition of Y, this is the case for each matching $\sigma' \notin Y$ that has been seen by MDB. Thus, assume that σ' was not seen.

Algorithm 7 The Matrix-Direct-with-Bounding (MDB) algorithm

1: Given m matchers, construct a new schema matcher with
2:    (a) similarity matrix M^* such that
3:      for $1 \leq i \leq n$, $1 \leq j \leq n'$, $M^*_{i,j} = H(M^{(1)}_{i,j}, \cdots, M^{(m)}_{i,j})$
4:    (b) local aggregator $h(\sigma, M^*)$.
5: $i = 1$
6: **repeat**
7:    Compute σ^*_i of M^* (using Algorithm 4)
8:    Obtain the actual weights $f^{(1)}(\sigma^*_i, M^{(1)}), \cdots, f^{(m)}(\sigma^*_i, M^{(m)})$
9:    Compute the aggregated weight $\langle \vec{f}, F \rangle(\sigma^*_i)$.
10:    **if** $\langle \vec{f}, F \rangle(\sigma^*_i)$ is one of the K highest seen so far **then**
11:      Remember σ^*_i
12:    **end if**
13:    $\tau_{MDB} = h(\sigma^*_i, M^*)$.
14:    $i \leftarrow i + 1$
15: **until** K matchings have been seen whose weight is at least τ_{MDB}
16: Let Y be a set containing K matchings with the highest grades seen so far.
17: **return** the graded set $\left\{ \left[\sigma, \langle \vec{f}, F \rangle(\sigma) \right] \mid \sigma \in Y \right\}$.

By the definition of τ_{MDB} as in step 13 of the MDB algorithm and the incrementality of Algorithm 4, for each such unseen σ' and for each $\sigma \in Y$, we have:

$$\langle \vec{f}, F \rangle(\sigma) \geq \tau \geq \langle h, H \rangle(\sigma') \geq \langle \vec{f}, F \rangle(\sigma')$$

where τ is the value of τ_{MDB} at termination of the MDB algorithm. The second inequality holds since σ' has not been seen and therefore $\langle h, H \rangle(\sigma')$ cannot receive a value higher than τ. Thus, we have proven that Y contains top-K matchings with respect to $\langle \vec{f}, F \rangle$.   □

Domshlak et al. [2007] show that, for schema metamatching, MDB can significantly outperform the Threshold algorithm. However, the Threshold algorithm can also significantly outperform MDB. This led to the design of the CrossThreshold algorithm, a hybrid version of these two algorithms, based on their in-parallel, mutually-enhancing execution.

5.4   SCHEMA MATCHING VERIFICATION

Gal [2006] introduced a second-line schema matcher that ensembles top-K matchings. It uses a simultaneous analysis of possible matchings to improve the matching outcome. This approach is in contrast to the common practice, in which ensembles use the best matchings of different matchers rather than the top-K matchings of a single matcher.

Given two schemata S and S', and a schema matcher, the schema matching verification (SMV for short) is described in Algorithm 8.

Algorithm 8 Schema Matching Verification

1: Generate a similarity matrix M
2: Generate top-K matchings $\{\sigma_1^*, \sigma_2^*, \ldots, \sigma_K^*\}$ using M and Algorithm 4.
3: **for** each attribute pair $\langle A_i, A_j \rangle$ **do**
4:      Generate a revised similarity matrix M' s.t. $M'_{i,j} \leftarrow$ Analyze $\{\sigma_1^*, \sigma_2^*, \ldots, \sigma_K^*\}$.
5: **end for**
6: **return** σ_1^*, computed using M' and Algorithm 4.

Under this generic methodology, a similarity matrix is generated and top-K matchings are generated and analyzed to identify attribute pairs that are worthy of further consideration (*i.e.*, verification). The algorithm then recomputes the similarity measures and generates the best matching.

Gal [2006] provided a concrete heuristic, instantiating the generic verification methodology presented earlier. Let S_1 and S_2 be two schemata and let M be a similarity matrix. Given a set $\{\sigma_1^*, \sigma_2^*, \ldots, \sigma_K^*\}$ of K top matchings and a user threshold $t \in [0, 1]$, the analysis step of the stability analysis heuristic first computes for each matrix entry the number of times it appears in $\{\sigma_1^*, \sigma_2^*, \ldots, \sigma_K^*\}$, dubbed $\iota_{i,j}$. It is worth noting that $0 \leq \iota_{i,j} \leq K$. Then, it generates a set of pairs $\{\langle A_i, A_j \rangle\}$ for which $\frac{\iota_{i,j}}{K} < t$. That is, the set contains all attribute pairs that do not appear a sufficient number of times in the top-K matchings, $\{\sigma_1^*, \sigma_2^*, \ldots, \sigma_K^*\}$. The recomputation phase revises G by setting $\varpi_{i,j} = 0$ for each such attribute pair.

Table 5.3: Stability analysis of the motivating example

S_1	S_2	$\frac{\iota(e)}{K}$
1	1	1.0
2	2	1.0
3	4	0.67
3	3	0.33
4	3	0.33
4	4	0.33

Example 5.15 Stability analysis example Consider Figure 5.1. Table 5.3 provides $\frac{\iota(e)}{K}$ values of all edges whose count in the top-3 matchings is non-zero, in decreasing order. For $t = 1$, the only non-zero edges will be those of the exact matching. □

For the stability analysis to work, a schema matcher should be monotonic. Under the assumption of a monotonic matcher, stable attribute matchings represent those matchings that are part of the exact matching. Empirical evaluation of stability analysis shows it to be effective [Gal, 2006], as detailed next.

Two schema matchers were used, namely **Term** and **Combined** (both monotonic), to generate the top-10 matchings. 86 Web forms were selected from different domains, including dating and matchmaking, job hunting, Web mail, hotel reservations, news, and cosmetics sales. Each Web form schema was extracted using OntoBuilder. Web forms were matched in pairs, where pairs were taken from the same domain. The schemata varied in size from 5 to 64 attributes, with about half the schemata having between 10 and 20 attributes. They also varied in the proportion of attribute pairs in the exact matching relative to the size of the schemata. This proportion ranged from 16.6% to 94.7%; the proportion in about half the schemata was more than 60%. The size difference between matched schemata ranged from no difference to about 3 times difference between schemata. In about half the pairs, the difference was less than 30%. Finally, the best matching precision results ranged from 5% to 100%, with about half the schema pairs matched with precision of more than 40%.

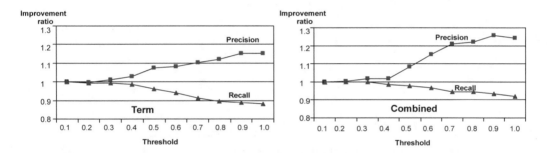

Figure 5.3: Precision and recall for stability analysis with $K = 10$

The independent variables of the experiments were K, the number of simultaneous matchings, and t, the threshold. Precision and recall were used for evaluation, measured for a fixed $K \in \{1, 2, ..., 10\}$, and varying the threshold t. Figure 5.3 presents the average change to precision and recall for different thresholds over all 43 real data pairs. K was set to 10. The left part of Figure 5.3 illustrates the results for the term matcher and the right part of Figure 5.3 for the combined matcher. In both cases, precision rises (in general) up to $t = 0.9$ with the increased threshold. Recall demonstrates a monotonic decrease with the increased threshold. This accords with intuition and is expected for monotonic matchers.

A closer look at the degree of improvement reveals that the precision of the term matcher rises by up to 15.4% (with $t = 0.9$). The combined matcher provides an increase of 25.6% (again with $t = 0.9$). As for recall, it decreases by a maximum of 11.9% for the term matcher and by a smaller 8% for the combined matcher (for $t = 1$). Therefore, stability analysis works better for the combined matcher than for the term matcher. This conclusion can be aligned with the empirical analysis of Gal et al. [2005a], where the exact matching was found, on average, at $K = 7$ for the combined matcher and at $K > 100$ for the term matcher.

Looking at the shape of the graphs, it appears that with both matchers, the improvement (in terms of precision) levels off at about $t = 0.9$. In general, the greater demand of a higher threshold benefits the heuristic up to a point, beyond which it becomes impossible for the top-K algorithm to keep even its stronger attribute correspondences. The "break-even point" depends to a great extent on the size of the schema, some evidence for which is given below. The term matcher has a more wiggly precision result, with some decrease in precision for $t = 0.1, 0.6$, and 0.7. Therefore, the performance of the term matcher is less predictable (although the difference is not statistically significant) than that of the combined matcher.

	Table 5.4: Stability analysis of ontology classes							
	Term				Combined			
	Precision		Recall		Precision	Recall		
Schema Class	Max Incr.	t	Max Decr.	t	Max Incr.	t	Max Decr.	t
Strongly Similar	19.8%	1.0	10.1%	1.0	28.5%	1.0	5.8%	1.0
Weakly Similar	12.1%	0.9	13.7%	1.0	23.3%	0.9	10.3%	1.0
Large	7.6%	1.0	8.5%	1.0	16.7%	1.0	3.6%	1.0
Small	20.7%	1.0	14.3%	1.0	29.5%	1.0	11.1%	1.0
Similar	8.9%	0.9	11.3%	1.0	19.9%	0.9	7%	1.0
Disimilar	24.1%	1.0	12.6%	1.0	32.3	0.9	9%	1.0
Low Initial Precision	11.4%	0.9	16.9%	1.0	27.6%	0.9	11.6%	1.0
High Initial Precision	19.2%	1.0	7.1%	1.0	24.5%	1.0	4.7%	1.0

Table 5.4 summarizes different ways of partitioning schema pairs according to various properties. A schema pair for which 60% or more of the attributes in one schema (called the target schema) can be matched to attributes in the other is considered to be *strongly similar*. 22 of the 43 pairs were strongly similar, with similarity ranging from 60% to 94.7%. K was set to 10. The results show improvement for strongly similar pairs over the whole group in the level of precision, with a small drop in recall. The precision of the term matcher was up to 19.8% higher for strongly similar pairs (with $t = 1$), while for the combined matcher, it increased by 28.5% (again with $t = 1$). Recall decreased by 10.1% for the term matcher and by a smaller 5.8% for the combined matcher. We can conclude from this that stability analysis works better for strongly similar ontologies.

A schema was defined to be large in this experiment if it had more than 20 attributes. There were 18 large target schemata. The results show less improvement in precision for larger schemata, but smaller decreases in recall. Precision increased by up to 7.6% for the term matcher and 16.7% for the combined matcher (with $t = 1$ in both cases). As for recall, it was lower by 8.5% for the term matcher and by 3.6% for the combined matcher. The smaller gain in precision and the smaller reduction in recall for larger schemata can be explained by the smaller marginal impact of a single attribute on the matcher's overall performance. Generally speaking, however, it seems that stability analysis is better suited for smaller schemata.

Schema pairs were considered similar if the number of attributes in the two schemata differed by less than 30% of the target schema (there were 23 such pairs). The results show less improvement in the precision level for similar-size schemata. The precision of the term matcher increased by up to 8.9% while that of the combined matcher rose by 19.9% (in both cases, with $t = 0.9$). Recall decreased by 11.3% for the term matcher and by 7% for the combined matcher. There is no obvious reason for this finding whereby stability analysis seems to be better suited for schema pairs that differ in size.

The last partitioning is based on the best matching precision level. Of the 43 pairs, 21 pairs with the term schema matcher and 20 pairs with the combined schema matcher had precision levels of less than 0.4 for the best matching. Here, the analysis shows different results for the two matchers. The stability analysis heuristic using the term matcher seemed to be more effective for pairs with high initial precision, increasing precision by an average of 19.2%. Using the combined matcher, the difference between the two groups was much smaller, showing slightly better performance (27.6% vs. 24.5%) for the ontology pairs with low initial precision. Recall, for both matchers, was significantly less affected by the stability analysis heuristic for schemata with high initial precision.

5.5   FINDING PROBABILISTIC ATTRIBUTE CORRESPONDENCES

In Section 3.3.2, we introduced a model for reasoning with uncertain schema matching using probabilistic attribute correspondences. Gal [2010] presents a method for deriving probabilistic attribute correspondences using top-K matchings. This work assumes that the probability that can be assigned to an attribute correspondence depends on two main factors. First, it depends on the degree of similarity that the matcher(s) of choice assign to this attribute correspondence. This is a natural assumption that lies at the basis of all matching techniques. Second, this probability also depends on the two attributes' ability to be matched together given the constraints of the matching task (modeled using the Γ function). To illustrate this point, consider example 3.1. R.CreditCardInfo.cardNumber can match well with both S.CreditCardInformation.cardNumber and S.HotelCardInformation.clientNumber. However, if the application enforces $1 : 1$ matching, then despite the high similarity that is assigned to both matches, they will have to "share" the same probability space when matched with R.CreditCardInfo.cardNumber.

Based on Section 5.3, given a user-defined K or a threshold on the minimum similarity, the system can produce alternative matchings and assign a probability estimate of correctness to each of them. The probability is based on the similarity measure, as assigned by an ensemble of matchers. To justify this method, we use the monotonicity principle, as discussed before.

Equipped with the monotonicity principle, one can generate a probability space over a set of K matchings, as follows. Let $(\varpi_1, \varpi_2, ..., \varpi_K)$ be the similarity measures of the top-K matchings $(\sigma_1, \sigma_2, ..., \sigma_K)$ and $\varpi_1 > 0$. The probability assigned to matching i is computed to be:

$$p_i = \frac{\varpi_i}{\sum_{j=1}^{K} \varpi_j}.$$

p_i is well defined (since $\varpi_1 > 0$). Each p_i is assigned a value in $[0, 1]$ and $\sum_{j=1}^{K} p_i = 1$. Therefore, $(p_1, p_2, ..., p_K)$ forms a probability space over the set of top-K matchings. For completeness, we argue that this probability space is appropriately considered a conditional probability, given that the exact matching is known to be within the top-K matchings.

We can create the probability of an attribute correspondence (A_i, A_j) by summing all probabilities of schema matchings in which (A_i, A_j) appears. That is, for a probabilistic attribute correspondence (A_i, A_j, p) we compute p to be:

$$p = \sum_{\sigma_l | (A_i, A_j) \in \sigma_l} p_l$$

The literature offers a few additional suggestions for using alternative matchings and assigning probabilities to attribute correspondences and matchings. Methods for assigning attributes to alternative schema matchings have also been suggested by other researchers, such as Magnani et al. [2005]. A method for deriving probabilities for schema matchings between a mediator and source schema is presented by Sarma et al. [2008]. Finally, a probabilistic lexical annotation technique for the generation of probabilistic attribute correspondences was suggested by Po and Sorrentino [2011].

CHAPTER 6

Applications

> *As we continue to improve our understanding of the basic science*
> *on which applications increasingly depend,*
> *material benefits of this and other kinds are secured for the future.*
>   – Henry Taube

In this chapter, we provide a set of applications where uncertain schema matching becomes handy. Section 6.1 provides an illustration of the use of uncertain schema matching within a project on a peer-to-peer data integration system. An application to disaster data management systems is discussed in Section 6.2. Section 6.3 looks at the use of uncertain schema matching in Web service discovery and composition. Finally, communities of knowledge are discussed in Section 6.4.

6.1   PEER-TO-PEER DATA INTEGRATION SYSTEMS

The European Future Internet initiative envisions small and medium businesses participating in value chains and networks that emerge dynamically as business needs evolve. Under this vision, the Internet will meet its promise to become a reliable, seamless and affordable collaboration and sharing platform. In principle, the ground is already laid for contemporary enterprises to be able to collaborate flexibly and affordably. However, businesses rarely share the same vocabulary and business semantics, raising the costs of B2B interoperability and collaboration. Small and medium enterprises cannot afford repeated data integration with new partners for ad-hoc collaboration, leaving the competitive advantage to large enterprises.

The NisB project (http://www.nisb-project.eu/) aims at easing ad-hoc data integration by harnessing the accumulative connectivity of the Web — the "evolving wisdom of the network." Much of this section draws upon the NisB Web site.

NisB can help lower the burden for second- and third-tier enterprises that have to deal with multiple heavy-weight and standard-setting enterprises in their value networks, and it can help groups of businesses entering a new industrial sector jointly leverage their interoperability efforts. NisB's novel contribution is its use of the network itself as a distributed repository and dispenser of the information and knowledge needed for data integration. The NisB approach allows businesses to share and reuse fragments of interoperability information (called *micro-mappings*) for the purpose of establishing user-centric understanding of diverse business schemata and vocabularies. Rather than limiting the heterogeneity of network members by forcing them to adopt some standardized solution or common ontology, the NisB system identifies and exploits bits and pieces of past experiences and practices which will be re-composed and orchestrated to solve new problems.

One of the main design principles of NisB is tolerance towards incomplete, erroneous, or evolving information, such as uncertain or erroneous micro-mappings and occasional changes in business schemata. Uncertainty is modeled along the lines outlined in Chapter 3, requiring no reference ontology and allowing decentralized control. Reasoning techniques (see Section 3.3), algorithmic solutions for ensembles (Chapter 4), and top-K matchings (Chapter 5) enable a pay-as-you-go approach to schema matching, where micro-mappings accumulate according to business needs without high upfront investment from individual network members while supporting quick setup for new members.

The research challenges of NisB cover four main areas. First, schema matchings are quantifiable using uncertainty analysis, so that users can be informed about the usefulness of reusing a matching. This approach promotes the sharing and reusing of fine-grain interoperability information. Second, schema matchings should make their way through the network, giving it enough context information to make them (re)usable. Third, the capabilities of domain experts should be analyzed to offer new methods for utilizing indirect feedback from users. This will empower users and reduce the time, effort, and expertise needed to establish interoperability. Finally, the use of top-K schema matchings should be extended. Together, resolving these challenges will lead to techniques and protocols for collaborative establishment of shared knowledge and understanding among communities of business users.

6.2   DISASTER DATA MANAGEMENT

Disaster management is part of the discipline of emergency management, which is aimed at both dealing with and avoiding emergency situations. By disaster management, we refer to the activities that take place after a disaster has occurred, including rescue and recovery. The term encompasses natural disasters (e.g., the 2005 hurricane Katrina), disease outbreaks (e.g., the 2003 SARS outbreak), major accidents (e.g., the 2010 Chilean mine collapse), and terrorism.

While disasters by definition affect the lives and the welfare of many individuals, they differ in their geographical impact and time scale. All disasters require immediate response, but in some cases, there is more time to establish an appropriate IT infrastructure than in others. Given this fact, a position paper by Naumann and Raschid [2006] identified the shortcomings of current IT solutions for disaster data management, highlighting the importance of reliable information integration and information sharing among the various bodies that must cooperate in disaster response: government agencies, NGOs, individuals, communities, and autonomous industry organizations. The discussion in this section follows closely the discussion in Naumann and Raschid [2006].

Disaster data management involves many different types of information, including data on victims and relief personnel; reports of damage to buildings, infrastructure and goods; weather forecasts; geographical data on roads and other landmarks; logistics of vehicles and delivery times; communications; details of aid and donations; and blog data. In disaster management, the difficulty of integrating autonomous, distributed, and heterogeneous data sources is compounded by severe time constraints and the ad-hoc nature of the process. While some planning for disasters can take place, it is impossible to predict all possible disasters and to know in advance who the potential participants will be. Indeed, participants may also change over the course of the disaster and the phases of disaster response. This renders any effort at manual a-priori integration futile [Naumann and Raschid, 2006].

Uncertain schema matching presents the most appropriate solution to the information integration challenges of disaster management, as outlined in Naumann and Raschid [2006]. The first challenge is to enable automated data integration, a direct outcome of the ad-hoc nature of the problem. Any fully automatic integration solution needs to quantify and accommodate the possibility of failure in integration. Therefore, a formal model of uncertainty (as proposed in Chapter 3) and tools such as top-K matchings (see Chapter 5) that provide alternatives to a correct mapping are needed. In addition, the diversity of data sources and user interfaces and their volatility suggest the importance of having multiple matchers, each handling different facets of the matching problem and assembled (see Chapter 4) to ensure the best possible matching outcome.

A second challenge involves the need for a flexible architecture, one that would facilitate dealing with frequent changes to individual sources as experts adapt available information systems to the demands of the particular disaster. Automatic schema matchings should therefore be quick, on the one hand, yet must remain within a given limit of accuracy. The use of uncertainty in schema matching allows such a tool.

A third challenge involves data quality. It is clear that poor data quality can squander resources and can even be life-threatening. Here, again, the ability to quantify the quality of a schema matching outcome has a direct impact on how well one can assess the quality of the generated data.

6.3   WEB SERVICE DISCOVERY AND COMPOSITION

Web services allow universal connectivity and interoperability of applications and services, using well-accepted standards such as UDDI, WSDL, and SOAP. Some Web services have semantic descriptions, anchoring them in an ontology, while others are only syntactically defined (using WSDL, for example). Designers can define a "virtual" Web service as part of their business processes, using a backend execution engine to look for actual Web services that match the specifications of the designer and can be invoked whenever the virtual Web service is activated.

Web services facilitate process integration. The REST protocol is a complementary representation of objects, based on the HTTP protocol. Just like Web services, REST is aimed at integration, focusing on integrating objects rather than processes.

To match the virtual Web service to actual Web services, data dependencies may be used, as well as the control structures in which process activities are organized. The distributed and independent nature of Web service development, and the lack of centralized control over vocabularies, suggests the need for uncertain schema matching techniques. Uncertainty that stems from concept mismatch can be managed through the use of schema matching algorithms, as described in chapters 4 and 5. Toch et al. [2005], for example, presented a Web service ranking that was extended to support imprecise matching by observing that an operation is expected to have input and output messages that match those of the virtual Web service. Therefore, matching Web service input and output parameters may carry with it a degree of uncertainty.

6.4   COMMUNITIES OF KNOWLEDGE

Communities of knowledge are groups of people who share information and knowledge as a means of self improvement and socializing. For example, the Rwandan Youth Information Community Organisation (rYico)[1] is a charitable organization that works to support and empower vulnerable young people in Rwanda by providing information centers that are of relevance to Rwandan youth and young adults.

A main challenge in this application is the auto-acquiring of the semantics of semi-structured and fully-structured pieces of information by educated non-experts to allow social media to improve the targeting of information. To do so, semantic schema matching should come into play (see Section 3.2.2). As mentioned before, semantic attribute correspondences can be modeled using the similarity matrix model and can be of practical value in matcher ensembles.

The information that streams into a community of knowledge should be automatically extracted, decomposed, unified, merged, and joined with information from other information sources. Towards this end, tools and algorithms for modeling uncertainty with semantic matchings and for schema matching of deep-Web documents should be developed. In such a setting, top-K queries à la Google would allow an educated community to reach decisions regarding the assignment of information to a community of knowledge and to generate rich semantic connections among information pieces.

---

[1] http://www.ryico.org/

CHAPTER 7

Conclusions and Future Work

> *A conclusion is the place where you get tired of thinking.*
> – Arthur Bloch

This manuscript has presented a thorough evaluation of uncertain schema matching. Starting from the basics of uncertainty, rooted in the AI literature, we proposed a model for uncertainty in schema matching. We then introduced two key tools for managing uncertainty, namely matcher ensembles and top-K matchings. We closed with a few applications where this theory can be applied.

Although work on uncertain schema matching has made huge strides forward in the past decade, there are several directions that require additional investigation. We detail three of them here.

The first challenge is to devise and evaluate quality models for the estimation of schema matchers. Precision, recall, and their derivatives have traditionally served the research community in offering ways to empirically test the performance of schema matchers. These metrics are explanatory in nature, measuring the goodness-of-fit of the heuristic to the data. The matrix abstraction can assist in the design of new, predictive metrics. Predictive measures typically measure the difference between some prediction as given by a model and the true outcome. We believe that relationships between a similarity matrix and matcher performance can be learned. Given a schema matcher and a matching generated by it, we would like to estimate the error encapsulated in this matching before having the exact matching at hand. Therefore, devising mechanisms for matcher self-assessment is a key direction for future research in this area.

The second challenge relates to the construction of ensembles. This topic of investigation, introduced by Gal and Sagi [2010], can be extended by formalizing the problem as a biobjective optimization problem: minimizing the ensemble size while maximizing improvement of performance (in terms of precision and recall). Therefore, the trade-offs inherent in adding and removing matchers from an ensemble (*e.g.,* two matchers that rank matchings identically should not both be included in an ensemble) can be learned.

The third challenge involves top-K matchings. We observed that top-K schema matchings play a pivotal role in managing uncertainty in schema matching. This research direction still has many open questions, the first of which is how top-K matchings can be identified in ensembles in polynomial time. The algorithms presented in Section 5.3 assume a uniform parallel querying of different matchers—that is, each iteration of the algorithm progresses on all the matchers. In general-purpose aggregation of quantitative rankings [Fagin et al., 2001], this strategy is indeed expected to be as good as any other. However, additional knowledge about the data may suggest (at least heuristically) better strategies. Also, the complexity of Algorithm 7 depends crucially on the quality of the chosen pair of dominating aggregators. Therefore, there is a need to refine the notion of dominance by incorporating topological measures of ordering and tightness.

These challenges and many others will enrich the research literature in the years to come. The area of uncertain schema matching is shaping up into a solid body of research, from theory to practice. As advances in the field join developments in other, closely related research areas in data integration, such as entity resolution, we believe the future holds greater automation and better solutions that will ensure the best possible data management.

Bibliography

S. Alagic and P.A. Bernstein. A model theory for generic schema management. In *Proc. 8th Int. Workshop on Database Programming Languages*, pages 228–246, 2001. DOI: 10.1007/3-540-46093-4_14 9

A. Algergawy. *Management of XML Data by Means of Schema Matching*. PhD thesis, Otto-von-Guericke University, 2010. 35

A. Anaby-Tavor. Enhancing the formal similarity based matching model. Master's thesis, Technion-Israel Institute of Technology, May 2003. 49

D. Barbosa, J. Freire, and A.O. Mendelzon. Designing information-preserving mapping schemes for XML. In *Proc. 31st Int. Conf. on Very Large Data Bases*, pages 109–120, 2005. 2, 29

C. Batini, M. Lenzerini, and S. Navathe. A comparative analysis of methodologies for database schema integration. *ACM Computing Surveys*, 18(4):323–364, December 1986. DOI: 10.1145/27633.27634 1, 18

M. Benerecetti, P. Bouquet, and S. Zanobini. Soundness of schema matching methods. In *Proceedings of the 2nd European Semantic Web Conference*, pages 211–225, 2005. DOI: 10.1007/11431053_15 9, 29

S. Bergamaschi, S. Castano, M. Vincini, and D. Beneventano. Semantic integration of heterogeneous information sources. *Data & Knowledge Engineering*, 36(3):215–249, 2001. DOI: 10.1016/S0169-023X(00)00047-1 1

J. Berlin and A. Motro. Autoplex: Automated discovery of content for virtual databases. In *Proc. Int. Conf. on Cooperative Information Systems*, pages 108–122. Springer, 2001. DOI: 10.1007/3-540-44751-2_10 1, 12, 17

P.A. Bernstein and S. Melnik. Meta data management. In *Proc. 20th Int. Conf. on Data Engineering*, 2004. Tutorial Presentation. DOI: 10.1109/ICDE.2004.1320101 1, 2

P.A. Bernstein, S. Melnik, M. Petropoulos, and C. Quix. Industrial-strength schema matching. *SIGMOD Record*, 33(4):38–43, 2004. DOI: 10.1145/1041410.1041417 17, 18, 31

P.A. Bernstein, S. Melnik, and J.E. Churchill. Incremental schema matching. In *Proc. 32nd Int. Conf. on Very Large Data Bases*, pages 1167–1170, 2006. 49

A. Bilke and F. Naumann. Schema matching using duplicates. In *Proc. 21st Int. Conf. on Data Engineering*, pages 69–80, 2005. DOI: 10.1109/ICDE.2005.126 64

P. Bohannon, W. Fan, M. Flaster, and P.P.S. Narayan. Information preserving XML schema embedding. In *Proc. 31st Int. Conf. on Very Large Data Bases*, pages 85–96, 2005. DOI: 10.1145/1331904.1331908 2, 29

S. Castano, V. De Antonellis, and S. De Capitani di Vimercati. Global viewing of heterogeneous data sources. *IEEE Trans. Knowl. and Data Eng.*, 13(2):277–297, 2001. DOI: 10.1109/69.917566 1

C.R. Chegireddy and H.W. Hamacher. Algorithms for finding k-best perfect matchings. *Discrete Applied Mathematics*, 18:155–165, 1987. DOI: 10.1016/0166-218X(87)90017-5 56

R. Cheng, J. Gong, and D.W. Cheung. Managing uncertainty of XML schema matching. In *Proc. 26th Int. Conf. on Data Engineering*, pages 297–308, 2010. DOI: 10.1109/ICDE.2010.5447868 2, 5

T.H. Cormen, C.E. Leiserson, and R.L. Rivest. *Introduction to Algorithms*. McGraw-Hill, New York, N.Y., 1990. 51

R. Dhamankar, Y. Lee, A. Doan, A.Y. Halevy, and P. Domingos. iMAP: Discovering complex mappings between database schemas. In *Proc. ACM SIGMOD Int. Conf. on Management of Data*, pages 383–394, 2004. DOI: 10.1145/1007568.1007612 17

H. Do, S. Melnik, and E. Rahm. Comparison of schema matching evaluations. In *Proceedings of the 2nd Int. Workshop on Web Databases (German Informatics Society), 2002.*, 2002. URL citeseer. nj.nec.com/do02comparison.html. DOI: 10.1007/3-540-36560-5_17 28

H.H. Do and E. Rahm. COMA - a system for flexible combination of schema matching approaches. In *Proc. 28th Int. Conf. on Very Large Data Bases*, pages 610–621, 2002. DOI: 10.1016/B978-155860869-6/50060-3 1, 14, 17, 33, 34, 35, 62

A. Doan, P. Domingos, and A.Y. Halevy. Reconciling schemas of disparate data sources: A machine-learning approach. In *Proc. ACM SIGMOD Int. Conf. on Management of Data*, pages 509–520, 2001. DOI: 10.1145/376284.375731 12, 17, 33, 41

A. Doan, J. Madhavan, P. Domingos, and A. Halevy. Learning to map between ontologies on the semantic web. In *Proc. 11th Int. World Wide Web Conf.*, pages 662–673, 2002. DOI: 10.1145/511446.511532 1

C. Domshlak, A. Gal, and H. Roitman. Rank aggregation for automatic schema matching. *IEEE Trans. Knowl. and Data Eng.*, 19(4):538–553, 2007. DOI: 10.1109/TKDE.2007.1010 14, 33, 60, 61, 65

X.L. Dong, A.Y. Halevy, and C. Yu. Data integration with uncertainty. In *Proc. 33rd Int. Conf. on Very Large Data Bases*, pages 687–698, 2007. DOI: 10.1007/s00778-008-0119-9 2, 5, 22, 26, 27

J. Drakopoulos. Probabilities, possibilities and fuzzy sets. *International Journal of Fuzzy Sets and Systems*, 75(1):1–15, 1995. DOI: 10.1016/0165-0114(94)00341-4 8

F. Duchateau, Z. Bellahsene, and R. Coletta. A flexible approach for planning schema matching algorithms. In *Proc. Int. Conf. on Cooperative Information Systems*, pages 249–264, 2008. DOI: 10.1007/978-3-540-88871-0_18 35, 48

C. Dwork, R. Kumar, M. Naor, and D. Sivakumar. Rank aggregation methods for the Web. In *Proc. 10th Int. World Wide Web Conf.*, pages 613–622, 2001. DOI: 10.1145/371920.372165 60

M. Ehrig, S. Staab, and Y. Sure. Bootstrapping ontology alignment methods with apfel. In *Proc. 4th Int. Semantic Web Conf.*, pages 186–200, 2005. DOI: 10.1007/11574620_16 36

D.W. Embley, D. Jackman, and L. Xu. Attribute match discovery in information integration: Exploiting multiple facets of metadata. *Journal of Brazilian Computing Society*, 8(2):32–43, 2002. DOI: 10.1590/S0104-65002002000200004 17, 18, 33

Jérôme Euzenat and Pavel Shvaiko. *Ontology matching*. Springer-Verlag, Heidelberg (DE), 2007. 18, 19, 20

R. Fagin. Inverting schema mappings. In *Proc. 25th ACM SIGACT-SIGMOD-SIGART Symp. on Principles of Database Systems*, pages 50–59, 2006. DOI: 10.1145/1292609.1292615 2

R. Fagin, A. Lotem, and M. Naor. Optimal aggregation algorithms for middleware. In *Proc. 20th ACM SIGACT-SIGMOD-SIGART Symp. on Principles of Database Systems*, pages 102–113, 2001. DOI: 10.1145/375551.375567 75

R. Fagin, A. Lotem, and M. Naor. Optimal aggregation algorithms for middleware. *Journal of Computer and System Sciences*, 66:614–656, 2003. DOI: 10.1016/S0022-0000(03)00026-6 60

R. Fagin, P.G. Kolaitis, L. Popa, and W.C. Tan. Quasi-inverses of schema mappings. In *Proc. 26th ACM SIGACT-SIGMOD-SIGART Symp. on Principles of Database Systems*, pages 123–132, 2007. DOI: 10.1145/1265530.1265548 2

W.B. Frakes and R. Baeza-Yates, editors. *Information Retrieval: Data Structures & Algorithms*. Prentice Hall, Englewood Cliffs, NJ 07632, 1992. 28

Y. Freund and R. Schapire. A short introduction to boosting, 1999. URL citeseer.ist.psu.edu/freund99short.html. 42

Y. Freund and R.E. Schapire. A decision-theoretic generalization of on-line learning and an application to boosting. *Journal of Computer and System Sciences*, 55(1):119–139, August 1997. DOI: 10.1006/jcss.1997.1504 43

A. Gal. On the cardinality of schema matching. In *IFIP WG 2.12 and WG 12.4 International Workshop on Web Semantics*, pages 947–956, 2005. DOI: 10.1007/11575863_116 21

A. Gal. Managing uncertainty in schema matching with top-k schema mappings. *Journal of Data Semantics*, 6:90–114, 2006. DOI: 10.1007/11803034_5 2, 17, 18, 35, 49, 65, 66, 67

A. Gal. Why is schema matching tough and what can we do about it? *SIGMOD Record*, 35(4):2–5, 2007. DOI: 10.1145/1228268.1228269 29

A. Gal. On enhancing the capabilities of attribute correspondences. In Z. Bellahsene, A. Bonifati, and E. Rahm, editors, *Schema Matching and Mapping*. Springer, 2010. 9, 26, 69

A. Gal and T. Sagi. Tuning the ensemble selection process of schema matchers. *Information Systems*, 35(8):845–859, 2010. DOI: 10.1016/j.is.2010.04.003 16, 42, 43, 45, 46, 75

A. Gal, A. Anaby-Tavor, A. Trombetta, and D. Montesi. A framework for modeling and evaluating automatic semantic reconciliation. *VLDB J.*, 14(1):50–67, 2005a. DOI: 10.1007/s00778-003-0115-z 2, 5, 6, 22, 29, 30, 31, 41, 68

A. Gal, G. Modica, H.M. Jamil, and A. Eyal. Automatic ontology matching using application semantics. *AI Magazine*, 26(1):21–32, 2005b. 1, 11, 12, 17, 19, 29, 33, 34

A. Gal, M.V. Martinez, G.I. Simari, and V.S. Subrahmanian. Aggregate query answering under uncertain schema mappings. In *Proc. 25th Int. Conf. on Data Engineering*, pages 940–951, 2009. 2, 5

Z. Galil. Efficient algorithms for finding maximum matching in graphs. *ACM Comput. Surv.*, 18 (1):23–38, March 1986. DOI: 10.1145/6462.6502 16

F. Giunchiglia, P. Shvaiko, and M. Yatskevich. Semantic schema matching. In *Proc. Int. Conf. on Cooperative Information Systems*, pages 347–365, 2005. DOI: 10.1007/11575771_23 20

T. Green and V. Tannen. Models for incomplete and probabilistic information. *Q. Bull. IEEE TC on Data Eng.*, 29(1):17–24, 2006. DOI: 10.1007/11896548_24 5

D. Gusfield and R.W. Irving. *The Stable Marriage Problem: Structure and Algorithms*. MIT Press, Cambridge, MA, 1989. 16

P. Hajek. *The Metamathematics of Fuzzy Logic*. Kluwer Acad. Publ., 1998. 6, 7

J.Y. Halpern. *Reasoning About Uncertainty*. MIT Press, 2003. 5

H.W. Hamacher and M. Queyranne. K-best solutions to combinatorial optimization problems. *Annals of Operations Research*, 4:123–143, 1985/6. DOI: 10.1007/BF02022039 56

B. He and K. Chen-Chuan Chang. Statistical schema matching across Web query interfaces. In *Proc. ACM SIGMOD Int. Conf. on Management of Data*, pages 217–228, 2003. DOI: 10.1145/872757.872784 11, 19

B. He and K.C.-C. Chang. Making holistic schema matching robust: an ensemble approach. In *Proc. 11th ACM SIGKDD Int. Conf. on Knowledge Discovery and Data Mining*, pages 429–438, 2005. DOI: 10.1145/1081870.1081920 12, 20, 33

R. Hull. Relative information capacity of simple relational database schemata. *SIAM J. Comput.*, 15 (3):856–886, 1986. DOI: 10.1137/0215061 29

E.P. Klement, R. Mesiar, and E. Pap. *Triangular Norms*. Kluwer Acad. Publ., 2000. 6

G.J. Klir and B. Yuan, editors. *Fuzzy Sets and Fuzzy Logic*. Prentice Hall, 1995. 6, 7, 22

B. Korte and J. Vygen. *Combinatorial Optimization: Theory and Algorithms*. Springer, second edition, 2002. 51, 52

S. Mac Lane. *Categories for the Working Mathematician*. Springer, second edition, 1998. 9

Y. Lee, M. Sayyadian, A. Doan, and A. Rosenthal. eTuner: tuning schema matching software using synthetic scenarios. *VLDB J.*, 16(1):97–122, 2007. DOI: 10.1007/s00778-006-0024-z 14, 17, 18, 22, 33, 35, 46

M. Lenzerini. Data integration: A theoretical perspective. In *Proc. 21st ACM SIGACT-SIGMOD-SIGART Symp. on Principles of Database Systems*, pages 233–246, 2002. DOI: 10.1145/543613.543644 1

H. Liu and H.-A. Jacobsen. Modeling uncertainties in publish/subscribe systems. In *Proc. 20th Int. Conf. on Data Engineering*, pages 510–522, 2004. DOI: 10.1109/ICDE.2004.1320023 6

J. Madhavan, P.A. Bernstein, and E. Rahm. Generic schema matching with Cupid. In *Proc. 27th Int. Conf. on Very Large Data Bases*, pages 49–58, 2001. 1, 11, 12, 14, 33

J. Madhavan, P.A. Bernstein, P. Domingos, and A.Y. Halevy. Representing and reasoning about mappings between domain models. In *Proc. 18th National Conf on Artificial Intelligence and 14th Innovative Applications of Artificial Intelligence Conf.*, pages 80–86, 2002. 2, 9, 29

J. Madhavan, P.A. Bernstein, A. Doan, and A. Halevy. Corpus-based schema matching. In *Proc. 21st Int. Conf. on Data Engineering*, pages 57–68, 2005. DOI: 10.1109/ICDE.2005.39 12, 20

M. Magnani and D. Montesi. A survey on uncertainty management in data integration. *ACM Journal of Data and Information Quality*, 2(1):1–33, July 2010. DOI: 10.1145/1805286.1805291 5

M. Magnani, N. Rizopoulos, P. McBrien, and D. Montesi. Schema integration based on uncertain semantic mappings. In *Proc. 24th Int. Conf. on Conceptual Modeling*, pages 31–46, 2005. DOI: 10.1007/11568322_3 2, 5, 70

A. Marie and A. Gal. On the stable marriage of maximum weight royal couples. In *Proceedings of AAAI Workshop on Information Integration on the Web*, 2007a. 12, 16

A. Marie and A. Gal. Managing uncertainty in schema matcher ensembles. In H. Prade and V.S. Subrahmanian, editors, *Scalable Uncertainty Management, First International Conference*, pages 60–73, 2007b. 13, 17, 33, 36, 39

A. Marie and A. Gal. Boosting schema matchers. In *Proc. Int. Conf. on Cooperative Information Systems*, pages 283–300, 2008. DOI: 10.1007/978-3-540-88871-0_20 33, 41

S. Melnik. *Generic Model Management: Concepts and Algorithms*. Springer-Verlag, 2004. 2

S. Melnik, H. Garcia-Molina, and E. Rahm. Similarity flooding: A versatile graph matching algorithm and its application to schema matching. In *Proc. 18th Int. Conf. on Data Engineering*, pages 117–140, 2002. DOI: 10.1109/ICDE.2002.994702 14, 34

S. Melnik, E. Rahm, and P.A. Bernstein. Rondo: A programming platform for generic model management. In *Proc. ACM SIGMOD Int. Conf. on Management of Data*, pages 193–204, 2003. DOI: 10.1145/872757.872782 1

E. Mena, V. Kashayap, A. Illarramendi, and A. Sheth. Imprecise answers in distributed environments: Estimation of information loss for multi-ontological based query processing. *Int. J. Cooperative Information Syst.*, 9(4):403–425, 2000. DOI: 10.1142/S0218843000000193 5, 28

R.J. Miller, Y.E. Ioannidis, and R. Ramakrishnan. The use of information capacity in schema integration and translation. In *Proc. 19th Int. Conf. on Very Large Data Bases*, pages 120–133, 1993. 29

R.J. Miller, L.M. Haas, and M.A. Hernández. Schema mapping as query discovery. In *Proc. 26th Int. Conf. on Very Large Data Bases*, pages 77–88, 2000. 2

R.J. Miller, M.A. Hernàndez, L.M. Haas, L.-L. Yan, C.T.H. Ho, R. Fagin, and L. Popa. The Clio project: Managing heterogeneity. *SIGMOD Record*, 30(1):78–83, 2001. DOI: 10.1145/373626.373713 1, 21

G. Modica, A. Gal, and H. Jamil. The use of machine-generated ontologies in dynamic information seeking. In *Proc. Int. Conf. on Cooperative Information Systems*, pages 433–448, 2001. DOI: 10.1007/3-540-44751-2_32 25, 28, 34, 64

P. Mork, A. Rosenthal, L.J. Seligman, J. Korb, and K. Samuel. Integration workbench: Integrating schema integration tools. In *Proc. 22nd Int. Conf. on Data Engineering Workshops*, page 3, 2006. DOI: 10.1109/ICDEW.2006.69 17, 33

K.G. Murty. An algorithm for ranking all the assignments in order of increasing cost. *Operations Research*, 16:682–687, 1968. DOI: 10.1287/opre.16.3.682 56

F. Naumann and L. Raschid. Information integration and disaster data management (DisDM). In *Online Proceedings of the Workshop on Information Integration*, 2006. http://db.cis.upenn.edu/iiworkshop/postworkshop/positionPapers/123.pdf. 72, 73

H. Nottelmann and U. Straccia. sPLMap: A probabilistic approach to schema matching. In *Proc. Advances in Information Retrieval, 27th European Conference on IR Research, ECIR 2005*, pages 81–95, 2005. DOI: 10.1007/978-3-540-31865-1_7 5

H. Nottelmann and U. Straccia. Information retrieval and machine learning for probabilistic schema matching. *Information Proc. & Man.*, 43(3):552–576, 2007. DOI: 10.1016/j.ipm.2006.10.014 17

M. Pascoal, M.E. Captivo, and J. Clímaco. A note on a new variant of Murty's ranking assignments algorithm. *4OR: Quarterly Journal of the Belgian, French and Italian Operations Research Societies*, 1(3):243–255, 2003. DOI: 10.1007/s10288-003-0021-7 56

L. Po and S. Sorrentino. Automatic generation of probabilistic relationships for improving schema matching. *Inf. Syst.*, 36(1):192–208, 2011. DOI: 10.1016/j.is.2010.09.004 70

H. Putnam. *Reason, Truth, and History*. Cambridge University Press, 1981. 29

E. Rahm and P.A. Bernstein. A survey of approaches to automatic schema matching. *VLDB J.*, 10 (4):334–350, 2001. DOI: 10.1007/s007780100057 1, 18

H. Roitman, A. Gal, and C. Domshlak. Providing top-k alternative schema matchings with *OntoMatch*. In *Proc. 27th Int. Conf. on Conceptual Modeling*, pages 538–539, 2008. DOI: 10.1007/978-3-540-87877-3_50 49

S. Ross. *A First Course in Probability*. Prentice Hall, fifth edition, 1997. 5, 14

K. Saleem, Z. Bellahsene, and E. Hunt. Performance oriented schema matching. In *Proc. 18th Int. Conf. Database and Expert Systems Appl.*, pages 844–853, 2007. DOI: 10.1007/978-3-540-74469-6_82 1

A.D. Sarma, X. Dong, and A.Y. Halevy. Bootstrapping pay-as-you-go data integration systems. In *Proc. ACM SIGMOD Int. Conf. on Management of Data*, pages 861–874, 2008. DOI: 10.1145/1376616.1376702 70

R. Schapire. The boosting approach to machine learning: An overview. In *MSRI Workshop on Nonlinear Estimation and Classification*, 2001. 41

R.E. Schapire. The strength of weak learnability. *Machine Learning*, 5:197–227, 1990. URL citeseer.ist.psu.edu/schapire90strength.html. DOI: 10.1023/A:1022648800760 41, 42

A. Sheth and J. Larson. Federated database systems for managing distributed, heterogeneous, and autonomous databases. *ACM Comput. Surv.*, 22(3):183–236, 1990. DOI: 10.1145/96602.96604 1

P. Shvaiko and J. Euzenat. A survey of schema-based matching approaches. *Journal of Data Semantics*, 4:146 – 171, December 2005. DOI: 10.1007/11603412_5 1

W. Su. *Domain-based Data Integration for Web Databases*. PhD thesis, Dept. of Computer Science and Engineering, Hong Kong Univ. of Science and Technology, Hong Kong, December 2007. 12

W. Su, J. Wang, and F. Lochovsky. A holistic schema matching for Web query interfaces. In *Advances in Database Technology, Proc. 10th Int. Conf. on Extending Database Technology*, pages 77–94, 2006. DOI: 10.1007/11687238_8 11, 12, 20

E. Toch, A. Gal, and D. Dori. Automatically grounding semantically-enriched conceptual models to concrete web services. In *Proc. 24th Int. Conf. on Conceptual Modeling*, pages 304–319, 2005. DOI: 10.1007/11568322_20 73

P. Valtchev and J. Euzenat. Dissimilarity measure for collections of objects and values. In *Advances in Intelligent Data Analysis, Reasoning about Data, Proc. 2nd Int. Symp.*, pages 259–272, 1997. DOI: 10.1007/BFb0052846 25

A.R. Vinson, C.A. Heuser, A.S. da Silva, and E.S. de Moura. An approach to xml path matching. In *Proc. 9th Int. Conf. on Web-Age Information Management*, pages 17–24, 2007. DOI: 10.1145/1316902.1316906 10

L.A. Zadeh. Fuzzy sets. *Information and Control*, 8:338–353, 1965. DOI: 10.1016/S0019-9958(65)90241-X 5, 6

Author's Biography

AVIGDOR GAL

Avigdor Gal is an Associate Professor at the Faculty of Industrial Engineering & Management at the Technion – Israel Institute of Technology. He received his D.Sc. degree from the Technion in 1995 in the area of temporal active databases. He has published more than 90 papers in journals (e.g., *Journal of the ACM* (JACM), ACM *Transactions on Database Systems* (TODS), IEEE *Transactions on Knowledge and Data Engineering* (TKDE), ACM *Transactions on Internet Technology* (TOIT), and the *VLDB Journal*), books (*Temporal Databases: Research and Practice, Schema Matching and Mapping*, and *Reasoning in Event-based Distributed Systems*) and conferences (ICDE, ER, CoopIS, BPM, DEBS) on the topics of data integration, complex event processing, temporal databases, information systems architectures, and active databases.

Avigdor is a member of CoopIS (Cooperative Information Systems) Advisory Board, a member of IFIP WG 2.6, and a recipient of the IBM Faculty Award for 2002-2004. He is a member of the ACM and a senior member of IEEE. Avigdor served as a Program co-Chair of CoopIS and DEBS, and in various roles in ER and CIKM. He served as a program committee member in SIGMOD, VLDB, ICDE and others. Avigdor was an Area Editor of the *Encyclopedia of Database Systems*.

Printed in the United States
by Baker & Taylor Publisher Services